ON THE AUTHORITY OF THE BIBLE

ON THE
AUTHORITY OF
THE BIBLE

Some Recent Studies

by

Leonard Hodgson

C. F. Evans

John Burnaby

Gerhard Ebeling

and

D. E. Nineham

LONDON

S·P·C·K

1960

First published in volume form in 1960
by S.P.C.K.
Holy Trinity Church
Marylebone Road
London N.W.1

Printed in Great Britain by
The Talbot Press (S.P.C.K.)
Saffron Walden, Essex

CONTENTS

PUBLISHER'S NOTE

THIS is intended to be the first of a series of publications bringing together in convenient and permanent form some of the occasional work of contemporary theologians. The importance of these collections will certainly not lie in any predetermined unity. None of them will have been in any sense planned as a symposium. In none of them will an editorial hand have played any but the most minor part. If they have importance it will rather be because they reveal what professional theologians, most of them teachers of theology, have had at the top of their minds when they were called upon to speak or to lecture on some given subject, or to offer an interim report of some actual pre-occupation. For in nearly every case the material of these studies will have been originally put together for a particular occasion, and in preparing them for publication, no attempt will have been made to conceal the circumstances of their composition.

Yet that they have been selected to form part of a volume will mean that they are thought to have more than occasional importance. For this reason some of them will be reprinted from periodicals in which they have already appeared. Moreover, because they are brought together as illuminating a single theme (although originally written quite independently, and although approaching that theme in quite different ways) it is hoped that they will be significant as collections; that they will show what are felt to be the pressing issues in a particular field of study. The purpose will therefore be to report, to inform, and to stimulate further study; and it is hoped that they will be of interest not only to scholars and students but also to those many who for various reasons, have no time for systematic study but are nevertheless interested in its progress.

It is not coincidence that this first volume bears upon the subject considered by Committee I of the Lambeth Conference 1958—*The Bible: its Authority and Message*. More than one of the Essays included was officially brought to the attention of the bishops preparing to meet in this Committee. This volume has the widest possible public in view; what it is concerned with is of fundamental importance for Christians of all communions. But the S.P.C.K., in publishing it at this time, admittedly hopes that it will not be least useful to those who are leading Anglican congregations in the ten years' study of the Bible commended by all the bishops at the Conference.

I

GOD AND THE BIBLE [1]

LEONARD HODGSON

I

As I read their writings, I get the impression that a large number of theologians to-day have not yet woken up to what has happened to the idea of revelation during the past hundred years, and to be conducting their theological discussions in dreamland, a dreamland in which we shall continue to go running round in circles until we have re-examined not only God's methods and channels of revelation but the very nature of revelation itself.

Look back with me to the turn of the century, to the days of my Victorian boyhood when men were seriously disturbed by the thought that any statement of fact in the Bible might be disproved by historical or scientific enquiry. Why were they so disturbed?

It is easy now to poke fun at the thought that the truth of the Christian faith depends on the world having been created in six days precisely as described in Genesis I. Why was it ever thought to be so? Why did contemporary works of Christian apologetics attempt to deal with the problem by arguing that if in the Hebrew mind the word translated "day" may have meant an indefinite period of time, the Genesis account could be reconciled with the scientifically discovered order of events?

The answer surely is that what was felt to be at stake was not the truth of this or that particular fact or set of facts, but the assurance of a divinely guaranteed revelation which was immune to the changes and chances of human discovery and criticism. From

[1] Reprinted from the *Church Quarterly Review*, Vol. CLIX, No. 333 (Oct.-Dec. 1958), pp. 532-46, and the *Bulletin* of the Berkeley Divinity School, U.S.A., No. 169 (June 1959).

I

that day to this Christian theology has been schizophrenic, one side of its mind pursuing paths of scholarship by methods of textual, grammatical. literary, historical, doctrinal, and philosophical enquiry, the other seeking to recover the sense of assurance that had been given by reliance on the divinely given revelation. On the scholarship side, for example, we see *Formgeschichte* supervene upon the Streeter type of gospel criticism; then the arrival of exegesis based on typological or liturgical considerations. These studies aim at increasing accuracy in exegesis, that is to say in the discovery of what the documents were meant to mean in the minds of their writers and were taken to mean by those for whom they were first written.

As a matter of scholarship this is, of course, important. Examiners rightly expect students not only to know the text of their documents but also to show some knowledge of current exegesis, of how Rawlinson, Lightfoot, and Farrer read St Mark, how Hoskyns, Dodd, Lightfoot, and Barrett read St John, how Cross and Mitton read Ephesians, how Selwyn and Beare read 1 Peter. All this, I repeat, is important as a matter of scholarship. My academic conscience, after many years as college tutor and university professor, makes me commend examiners who demand a high standard of accurate knowledge and intelligent discussion in this field as a necessary qualification for high honours in theology. But then up speaks the other side of my theological mind. This cannot be all that there is to it. This is just the same kind of knowledge as is required by examiners for honours in classics, history, philosophy, politics, English or foreign languages and literature, and other secular subjects. There must be something more, something in virtue of which we call our subject theology, as being the study of what in some distinctive way is a matter of divine revelation.

"In some distinctive way." Consciously or unconsciously, for half a century or more, we have been feeling around for an answer to the question "In what way?" What are we to put in the place of the pre-critical acceptance of the Bible as a divinely guaranteed manual of information about matters too high for scrutiny by human reason? I have said a good deal about this in my Gifford Lectures, and will not go over that ground again now.[2] I will add one comment on the present situation.

2 *For Faith and Freedom*, Vol. I. Lecture IV; Vol. II. Lecture I.

I have mentioned a few commentaries on certain books of the New Testament, confining my list to a small number of those written in English. Add to these the many others from Great Britain, France, Switzerland, Germany, Scandinavia, and elsewhere. Here is the New Testament, one little corpus of twenty-seven comparatively short books. And here is this vast and growing library of commentaries, growing because in every generation there arise theologians who feel themselves called upon to add to the number. What do they think they are doing beyond increasing the material for exploitation by examiners and their victims?

I have a strong suspicion that to a large extent these efforts are unconsciously motivated by the notion that if only we could get back to what the inspired author had in mind, and meant his reader to understand by what he wrote, we should have reached the goal of our quest for what is to be for us the *vox Dei*. What has happened in the nineteenth and twentieth-century history of theology is that we have substituted for the pre-critical acceptance of biblical statements as they stand a hypothetical acceptance of what the various biblical authors may ultimately be proved to have meant. We cling to the conviction that somewhere there is to be found a statement of revealed truth which is simply to be accepted as above and immune to criticism. With one side of our mind we continue to probe for it by methods of scholarly research. With the other, in spite of the fact that this scholarship does not stand still, that almost every day some scholar proposes some new line of exegesis, we pretend to ourselves that we have it in something called biblical theology. The Lady Theology, once called the Queen of the Sciences, is suffering from schizophrenia.

We shall never cure her so long as we cling to this notion that somewhere there is to be found a statement of truth which is to be regarded as immune to criticism, for this is the fathering upon God of the kind of revelation that we feel we would have given if we had been in his place. To quote from my Giffords:

"We walk by faith, not by sight." False theories of revelation spring from a refusal to be content with our creaturely status, an insistence that the only revelation worth having is one which gives us the kind of knowledge open only to a spectator of all time and all existence. But it is not for us to dictate to our Creator. We must be content to see and think and speak as men of our own age and culture. The measure of our faith in Him is our willingness to walk by the light of the kind of revelation that He has thought fit to give us.[3]

That revelation is given primarily not in words but in deeds, in events which become revelatory to us as the Holy Spirit opens our eyes to see their significance as acts of God. He reveals himself in his creative activity, and all that we can learn of the nature of the universe by scientific research or otherwise is a channel through which he reveals himself in the manner of his creation. For us Christians the Bible bears witness to a series of events in the history of mankind in which he reveals himself in his redemptive activity.

Our grasping of the significance of these events inevitably involves verbal statement. We human beings are so made that we can only think in words, unuttered words they may be, spoken to ourselves without realizing that we are so doing, but words, nevertheless, and words which are coloured by the thought-forms and linguistic usage of our age and culture.

This is why it is important to distinguish between the substance of the revelation, the acts of God, and the accounts which are given of their occurrence and their significance. Here let me quote from what I have written before in criticism of the statement that "since all subsequent theologies stand as an interpretation of the original *kerygma*, it is by the faithfulness to the *kerygma* that they must be judged".

> The mistake here is to identify the revelation itself, the *depositum fidei*, with some verbal expression of it. It would be more accurate to say that all subsequent theologies must be judged by their faithfulness to the revelation of God in Christ to which the primitive *kerygma* bore witness. . . .
>
> Careful exegesis of the text, seeking to understand what it meant in the minds of its original writers and readers, must be the basis of all attempts at exposition or the formulation of doctrine. But then the further question has to be asked: "What must the truth have been if it appeared like this to men who thought like that ?" St. Peter saw it with the eyes of a Palestinian Jew who up to the Day of Pentecost had not, so far as we know, travelled further from Galilee than Jerusalem; St. Paul, a Pharisee who had been born a Roman citizen, after his schooling by Gamaliel had had a university education at Tarsus; St. John (if Dr. Dodd is right) had a mind at home in the Hellenistic

[3] Vol. I, p. 89.

culture of Ephesus. If truth about God's revelation be such that those men saw it and wrote of it like that, what must it be for us?[4]

The *depositum fidei*, the enduring element which persists through all the history of Christian doctrine, is given by what God has *done* in the history of this world. In this lies the firm foundation of our faith, unchanging and unchangeable because (as Aristotle reminds us in the words of an old Greek poet)[5] even God cannot alter the fact that what has been done has been done. But the firmness of the foundation is not the same kind of firmness that we used to think we had, and we shall not be cured of our schizophrenia until we are cured of our subconscious hankering after what God has not thought fit to give us.

2

The title "God and the Bible" expresses my conviction that without realizing what we are doing we are trying to put the Bible in the place of God. This is one form of what comes from demanding the kind of revelation we think we ought to have been given. There are others, for example the doctrine of papal infallibility. A Roman Catholic writer is quoted by a reviewer as writing: "Without a teacher who can tell us, beyond the possibility of error, which of the various meanings is Christ's, we should have no revelation but only an ever growing pile of conundrums."[6] What links together the various forms of this error is the delusion that if we are to have a revelation worth having we must be able to find an ultimate source of authority somewhere within creation. In whatever form it appears it must be resisted: it is idolatry to credit any creature with what belongs to God alone.

The Roman Catholic fears that if he cannot rely on the Pope for his ultimate authority, he will have "no revelation, but only an ever growing pile of conundrums". We feel ourselves to be in like case. For us the ever growing spate of biblical commentaries is an ever growing pile of conundrums. What can we say positively about the kind of revelation that God has thought fit to give us and of the place of the Bible in it?

[4] *For Faith and Freedom*, Vol. II, pp. 227-8.
[5] *Eth. Nic.* 1139 b.
[6] F. J. Sheed. See *Theology*, October 1958, p. 432.

We start from the fundamental principle that the only ultimate source of authority is God: the living God, the eternal God, God the same yesterday, to-day, and for ever. The word "revelation" is a noun denoting what God is revealing. I say "is revealing" rather than "has revealed", because while we are creatures of space and time who "look before and after", the activity of the eternal God must be thought of as in the eternal timeless present. God is revealing himself to man. Man has to receive the revelation as it appears to him at each particular stage of his own history in time. This revealing is an educative process, and our experience of education gives us an analogy that makes the point clear. In relation to his pupils a teacher may be said in a sense to be eternal, to transcend the course of their progress in time. To begin with he has in his mind more both of fact and of understanding than they can assimilate. As he wills to communicate it to them he knows that he must wait upon the growth of their capacity to receive what he has to give. As he reads their essays and their examination papers he notes with joy all evidence of their intelligently grasping what he is trying to open their eyes to. As they themselves in later years re-read what they had then written, they may say: "This is how what we now understand more fully looked to us then."

The history of human thought is the history of God's revelation, God stripping off from the minds of men successive layers of misconception which miscolour their reception of what he is seeking to reveal. Progress in the fields of secular knowledge is progress in the grasping of what God is revealing through his creative activity. Progress in specifically Christian theology is progress in grasping what God is revealing through his redemptive activity, that series of events in the history of this world which we Christians see as acts of God at work within his creation to rescue it from the evil with which it had become infected. The importance of the Bible lies in its being the medium through which we see and grasp the significance of these mighty acts of God. The climactic centre is Christ incarnate, his birth, ministry, crucifixion, resurrection, ascension, and his giving of the Spirit to recommission the remnant of God's chosen people as the Christian Church. This is set in its historical context. Rightly to lay hold on him as a figure in actual history we have to see how the events of the New Testament develop from what led up to them, and how they in turn throw back light on the

Old Testament as the preparatory stage in God's redemptive work. Rightly to grasp his significance for theology we have to see the whole of subsequent history as the working out of what was done "in that dark noontide hour". The uniqueness of the Bible lies in the uniqueness of the events which constitute the redemptive activity of God. "Once, only once, and once for all his precious life he gave."

The acts embodied in events which constitute God's creative and redemptive activity are taken up into his revelatory activity in his action through the Holy Spirit "who spake by the prophets". He opens the eyes of men to see the significance of events as divine acts revelatory of God. It is here that the reception by man in time of what the eternal God is revealing takes the form of a developing educative process. It is one aspect of the infection of creation by evil that in the life of each one of us, as also in the lives of men in groups and of mankind as a whole, education has to proceed by the stripping away of misconceptions which miscolour our apprehension of the truth. The events which embody God's redemptive activity are known to us through the biblical writers. By the guidance of the Holy Spirit those of the Old Testament see the history of Israel as God at work calling and commissioning his people and preparing them for the mighty work which in his own good time he will perform. The New Testament writers see in Jesus Christ the fulfilment of these promises of God. They put down what they see and pass it on to us, and what was revelation to them becomes revelation to us as the Holy Spirit opens our eyes to see through their eyes and to see what they saw.

But it becomes a revelation with a difference. The Old Testament writers saw what they saw with the eyes of men in their grade in God's Divinity School. Those of the New Testament were Palestinian Jews and men of the Hellenistic world at the beginning of our era. We are western Europeans and Americans of the twentieth century, A.D. We need all the help we can get from theological scholarship to enable us to see as clearly and accurately as we can through the eyes of those on whose witness we depend. But we have to look as men of our own age and culture, trusting in the Holy Spirit to guide us as we seek to discount whatever in their vision was miscoloured by the misconceptions of their age and to grasp whatever new insights he may have in store for us as he fulfils our Lord's promise that he will lead us into all truth.

So I come to the suggestion I want to make towards the healing of our theological schizophrenia. It is that for rescue from being at the mercy of a pile of conundrums we should cease to look for an ultimate source of authority anywhere within creation, and realize that what the situation calls for is a deeper and more active faith in God himself. God alone is the ultimate source of authority. Whatever claim the councils of the Church, or the Bishop of Rome, or the biblical writers, or their scholarly expositors may have to speak in his name is a claim to be used by him as media for the communication of what he wills to make known to men.

At first hearing this sounds like nothing more than a pretentious platitude. "Of course", it will be said, "that is what we have always held. The use of the phrase 'God's word' shows that, for a word is simply a medium for the speaker's self-expression." But this misses the point of what I am trying to say. The question is whether God has given to his biblical word a kind of independent substantial existence so that it can operate on its own apart from his continued activity. I can perhaps make the point clear by reference to another discussion in which the same issue is raised. Sometimes language is used which suggests that God's grace is given to man as something with a similar independent existence, like the medicine which the doctor gives to a patient to be taken three times a day. I am urging that whatever may be said in criticism of that way of thinking of God's grace should be applied equally to similar thinking about God's biblical word. When I say that what is needed is a deeper and more active faith in God I mean faith in God as he is living and active and seeking to speak to us here and now to-day. Our question is not "What does the Bible say?" but "What is God now using the Bible to say?"

We must not minimize the danger of the "pile of conundrums". We must face the fact that the suggestion I am making opens the door to the possibility of widespread confusion by the scope it gives to the subjective element in our receiving of revelation. If as I read a passage in the Bible I am to be asking "What is God now trying to say to me through my reading of this written word?" how am I to guard against my reading into it what I am predisposed to find, so that my hearing of God's word expresses the content of my own mind rather than that of his? So long as the subject-matter of our research is provided by evidence concerning things within creation, evidence which is public and open to all to see, its public and open character acts as a check on the subjectivity of individual scholars. Where can we look for a similar check on the subjectivity of individual prophets who look up from the pages of their Bibles saying "Thus saith the Lord"?

This is the first of two problems presented to us theologians to-day. My present aim is to expose it, not to make any claim to have solved it. There is much work still to be done before we shall be in a position to see clearly what is to take the place of the kind of reliance on the Bible which was possible for our forefathers, and it is one of the obligations of true scholarship that we should resist the temptation to make premature claims. But before I end I must try to give some indication of lines on which I hope it may be possible to advance.

In our quest for objectivity we have a twofold source of help. First, as the foundation of everything, there must be our faith in God, in the living God, the faithful and true, the same yesterday, to-day, and for ever, who wills us to grow in knowledge of himself and of his will for us. Then secondly, there is the contribution of theological scholarship, accepted as a gift of God, given to be one of the channels of his self-revelation. It is, I think, beginning to be possible to see how these may work in together.

If we really and truly believe that God is one, that he is faithful and true, that he is educating man in knowledge of himself, that he is not only doing this in his creative activity through our secular learning but is also giving us the key to the understanding of all things in his redemptive activity which is the province of Christian theological study, then we can see how this study may act as a check on our subjective imaginings, and help us towards the objectivity we desire. For if God is one and is faithful and true there will be a self-consistency in his self-revelation. As we look back over his education of our spiritual ancestors our aim is to distinguish at each stage of the process genuine insights from wild speculations, lapses into bypaths of error, and misconceptions due to their seeing with the eyes of their age and culture and, it may be, their personal idiosyncrasies.

It is the function of scholarship, in the narrower and stricter sense of the word, to ensure that our understanding of the history of Christian thought shall be as objectively accurate as we can make it. Herein lies the importance of linguistic and textual studies, of efforts to set the works of any writer in the context of contemporary happenings and thought, to discover the cast of his own mind, to trace the sources from which his thought has been influenced, and to plot the course of its own development. Here we are dealing with evidence which is public and open to all, and as various scholars study it from various angles, publish their findings, and argue and discuss with one another, there is built up as near an approach to objective judgement upon it as here on earth we have any right to expect. In our biblical studies we are trying to see as clearly as we can what has actually been done by God in the history of this world in his redemptive activity. Then, set free from the obsession that we are looking to past ages for some finally authoritative statement of what we are to think to-day, we see God's education of man continued as the Holy Spirit takes of the things of Christ and opens the eyes of successive generations of Christians to grow in understanding the significance of what he has been and done. In this, as I have said, our aim is to disentangle genuine insights from misconceptions. Here again such objectivity as we have a right to expect will come as a result of scholars putting alongside of one another their various readings of the evidence, each saying to the rest: "This is how I see it. Cannot you see it too?"

When we turn to the subjective side, thinking about ourselves as seeking to receive God's revelation, we have to distinguish between the theological and the devotional use of the Bible. These are both referred to in the Report of the 1958 Lambeth Conference: "The great Christian doctrines are . . . interpretations of the Biblical drama", and "All should read the Bible as nourishment for the soul".[7] Perhaps I can best explain what I want to say by giving illustrations of actual attempts to discover what God is seeking to say to us to-day.

First, for the bearing of theological study on the doctrinal interpretation of the biblical drama, consider the relation of the Church to the world.

When Christianity began it was taken for granted by everyone that religion exists for the benefit of religious people, that a religious

[7] *The Lambeth Conference 1958.* Part 2, pp. 2, 12, 14.

body exists for the benefit of its members. It was not only that the Jews thought in this way about being the "chosen people". In the live religions of the Hellenistic world men were initiated into the mysteries in order to participate in the benefits promised to the initiates. When St Peter preached the first Christian sermon and exhorted his hearers to repent and be baptized into the Christian Church for the remission of their sins, this was inevitably taken to be an invitation to join a body which had a superior status in relation to God, which was being rescued for eternal bliss out of the perishing world. It would be unreasonable to expect either St Peter or his hearers to have thought of it in any other way.

Twenty centuries of Christian theology have not as yet succeeded in getting this notion out of our minds. It still inspires numberless evangelistic crusades, and books and reports of Church committees on evangelism. Yet this century's study of the gospels shows it to be inconsistent with the revelation of God in Christ. The sheer impact of historical study has erased the picture of Jesus as a human ethical and religious teacher who made no claims on his own behalf to any supernatural status. We have come to see that we cannot read the New Testament in its context in contemporary Jewish literature without seeing that at the heart of our Lord's thought about himself, from which spring all his deeds and his words, was the conviction that he was called to be God's Messiah holding—in whatever particular sense you interpret that title and that vocation—a unique status in relation to both God and man. "He came unto his own and his own received him not." They could not recognize in him the Messiah because he would not be the kind of Messiah they looked for. He would not "take his power and reign". He came not to be ministered unto but to minister, to empty himself and take the form of a servant, to give his life a ransom for many. We have come to see, too, that as a matter of history the Christian Church did not come into existence by the banding together of the individual disciples of a revered teacher; but was commissioned to be the messianic community by the Lord who knew himself to be the Messiah. All this is now common stock of our theological teaching. But have we begun to realize how deeply our current idea of evangelism reflects an idea of the Church which is inconsistent with the revelation of God in Christ, that the revolution which he wrought in the idea of messiahship involves a parallel revolution in the idea of the messianic community, the Church; that we should not think of being baptized into the Church as meaning being gathered into the company of the saved, but as being enlisted in the body in and through which the crucified, risen, and ascended Messiah wills to continue his working for the rescue of God's creation from all that prevents it from reflecting and manifesting the glory and beauty and majesty of its Creator?

When we follow out this line of thought we find that we have to consider further how we are to think about God himself. If what I have been saying is true of the Church, we cannot think of God in a way that implies that he is only interested in saving a certain number of souls out of this perishing world while the rest are scrapped. We shall have to relate our doctrine of redemption to a more articulate doctrine of creation, one that thinks of God as interested in all that makes for the glory and beauty of the world of his creation and for the welfare of his creatures. We must relate our concern for our sins to his call to us to share in his interests and to give ourselves to their service, asking for pardon and cleansing because our pride, our laziness, our cowardice, and selfishness and all the rest of them hamstring our response to his call to lose sight of ourselves in our care for the things that he cares for.

To illustrate the devotional use of the Bible, imagine a man who has reached the position to which we have now come in this lecture, who reads the Bible as one who is asking what God is now using the Bible to say to him to-day. Imagine this man to be reading the fourth chapter of Romans in which Abraham is commended for his faith in believing the angelic promise of a son against all the evidence provided by his own and Sarah's age. What is he to make of this? St Paul apparently not only took the story of Abraham as literal history, but regarded it as evidence that Abraham made the kind of response that God looked for. Are we to conclude that God sets a premium on this kind of credulity and looks for it in us?

Now imagine that for some time this man's mind has been haunted by a nagging doubt concerning his whole faith in God. He looks back to the days of his youth, that optimistic first decade of this century, when to Christians both in England and America Tennyson's "divine event to which the whole creation moves" did not seem so far off after all, when the Student Christian Movement and the Student

Volunteer Missionary Union took for their slogan "the evangeliza-
tion of the world in this generation". He sees a very different world
to-day. There has been no steady progress to world-wide peace and
brotherhood with conversion to Christianity and enlightened liberal-
ism. There has apparently been no progress, steady or otherwise,
towards a universal acceptance of Christian values; both at home and
abroad they seem to be in danger of being submerged under a rising
tide of secularism. Instead of the world having been evangelized in
his generation the nascent forces of nationalism are stimulating a
recrudescence of missionary activity by Muhammadans, Buddhists,
and Hindoos. How can we believe that God really cares for the
coming of his kingdom and the doing of his will on earth as it is in
heaven? Does not all the evidence go to show that we should revert
to the belief that he is only interested in the rescue of a certain
number of souls out of the perishing universe and has given us the
Bible as a manual of instruction for those that are to be saved?

Then he remembers the ground on which he has been driven to
reject that way of thinking of God and of the Bible, and how to go
back to it for the sake of peace of mind would be an act of intellectual dishonesty, a betrayal of his faith in God as the God of truth and
in Jesus Christ as the revelation of God. So he hears God saying to
him that though Abraham may have been no historical figure and
though his faith may be represented in the story as a credulity un-
becoming to a Christian of to-day, yet still there are occasions when
a man must show his faith by clinging to what he honestly believes
to be true in spite of evidence that tells against it. He hears it as a
call to strengthen his trust in God, to challenge the spirit of fear that
besets him in the name of the God whose gift is power and love and
a sound mind. So from his reading and meditation he goes forth
with strength renewed.

Do what we will, we cannot get away from the fact that as a man
reads he will hear the message that his mind is predisposed to find.
It is no good trying to evade this fact. We have got to accept it and
face it. When we accept it and face it we begin to see how different
members in the body of Christ may work together for the building
up of the whole in love. It is the responsiblility of the theologians to
discipline their minds and their studies so as to ensure, as far as is
possible, that the doctrinal interpretation of the biblical drama shall
give genuine insight into the objective truth that God is seeking to

reveal. What the great majority of Christians will find in the Bible, simple believers to whom God has given neither a vocation to theological study nor aptitude for it, will depend on the doctrinal presuppositions with which they come to it. Here lies the opportunity for all whose ministry is of a pastoral character in parish or school. If the theologians are rightly dividing the word of God, and the pastors and teachers are predisposing the minds of their flocks in accordance with their insights, God will be able to use the Bible to speak home to all, both for the deepening of our understanding and the nourishment of our souls.

3

If our Christian gospel be the proclamation of what God has done in Christ in the history of the world, its truth will depend on the historical truth of the events which we proclaim as acts of God. Here is the second problem for twentieth-century theologians.

In his survey of the history of catholic thought from Bossuet to Newman, Dr Owen Chadwick shows theologians haunted by the fear of having to build their faith on the shifting sands of historical probabilities, turning this way and that in the search for an impregnable rock, seeking it now in the dogmatic definitions of Councils, now in the authority of the Church, now in the infallibility of the Pope. Bultmann's existentialist theology carries on the tale : for the foundation of our faith the uncertainties of history can be transcended by reliance on the certainty of a present relationship between the soul and God. For Tillich "revealed truth lies in a dimension where it can neither be confirmed nor negated by historiography. . . . Although it is mediated primarily through historical events, (it) does not imply factual assertions, and it is therefore not exposed to critical analysis by historical research."[7] There are passages in Professor Ramsey's book on *Religious Language* which seem to me to tend in the same direction. About half-way through his *Mystery and Philosophy*, without explaining what he means by it, Mr M. B. Foster introduces the idea of revelation as a kind of *deus ex machina* immune to historical criticism. All these illustrate the working of the assumption that somehow or other, somewhere or other, there must be a sub-stratum of revealed truth which is immune to human criticism.

The need to be rescued from the illusion that God must have given the kind of revelation we think he ought to have given has relevance to every field of human inquiry, to questions scientific, philosophical, moral and aesthetic as well as historical. It is with the historical that we are now concerned. Here we cannot have it both ways. We cannot both proclaim our gospel as the good news of what God in Christ has actually done in the history of this world of space and time and also claim that our account of his doings is immune to historical criticism.

I have been showing how we theologians are beset by the temptation to evade this question, to try to find some foundation for our faith which will save us from having to face it. I want now to express my indebtedness to Professor John McIntyre of Edinburgh for the help that is given in his book *The Christian Doctrine of History*. It may not be the last word on the subject; it is a pioneering work which is pioneering in the right direction, which has seen what is the question that must be faced and sets out to try to face it. In what follows I am pursuing a train of thought set in motion by the reading of this book.

What is history? We have passed beyond the notion, fairly widespread at one time, that we can keep apart so-called facts and their interpretation, that the task of the historian is first to establish, as a matter of scientific certainty, the bare facts and then to discuss their interpretation. We have come to see that the so-called fact and interpretation are far more closely, are inextricably intertwined. McIntyre defines history as "meaningful occurrence", and argues that, if an occurrence has a meaning, that meaning is as intrinsic an element in the objective fact as the occurrence in which it is embodied. But our capacity to perceive meanings is affected by the categories with which our minds are equipped for their understanding. It is not a matter of our imposing a subjective interpretation on objectively ascertained facts. The question is whether the categories with which we are working are such as to enable us rightly to appreciate objectively meaningful occurrences.

Look at it like this. Imagine yourself to be a materialist of a kind which flourished about the end of the last century, one who holds that the only reality is the sequence of events in the physico-chemical world to be understood by the scientific study of causes and effects. For you history will be the record of what is at bottom the operation of these causes, all human thoughts and feelings and aspirations and our illusory sense of freely willed activity being epiphenomena, sensations generated and thrown off in the ongoing process of physico-chemical causation.

Now imagine yourself to be a humanist. You bring in a second factor. Human thoughts, feelings, aspirations, and purposively willed actions have a reality of their own. History is the record of events which embody the interactions of two factors, the sequence of cause and effect in the physical world and the purposive activity of men and women.

Imagine, thirdly, that you are a theist, a believer in God. Now you have a third factor to take into account, God's providential control of the world to which he has given the dependableness of the causal order and the human power of purposive action. To grasp the meaning of any event in history, to know what it was as a matter of objective, historical fact, it must be seen as one in which these three factors intertwine and interact.

So, lastly, look out from the standpoint of a Christian. God is not only the Creator of the universe who has given us the dependableness of the physical world and our own freedom and exercises his providential control over it all. He is the God who has entered personally into our history and lived as a man. If this be true, here is a fourth factor to be taken into account, a factor of such stupendous significance that it will affect our understanding of everything in space and time. Affect our understanding, do I say? That is only secondary. *If it be true* it will affect our understanding because it has affected the nature of that which we are seeking to understand. Our understanding will only be correct understanding in so far as we take into account this factor as itself objective matter of fact, as entering into and constituting the very stuff of history.

If the Christian gospel be true the events with which it is concerned are such that in our study of history we have to take into account both God's providential control of his creation and his living a human life at a particular time and place in the history of this world. This involves the consideration of questions to which it is impossible for any human being to know the answers. Take, for example, some of those which arise out of belief in the resurrection of Christ. Because we believe the events of the first Good Friday and

Easter Eve to have been the passing from earthly life of God incarnate we can accept as matters of history the disappearance of the earthly body and the finding of the empty tomb on Easter Day. But if we are asked to give a more detailed account, in terms of chemistry or physics, of what happend to the earthly body, or of the nature of the risen body, or of how we think the one became the other, then we have to be content to say that this is the kind of question to which no man knows the answer. We have to be content to be like the man born blind, whose inability to give an account of the process of his healing did not affect the historicity of the event in the history of his life to which he bore witness: "Whereas I was blind, now I see." Our inability to give an account of the process of transformation does not affect our faith that our risen Lord, he who holds in his hands the destinies of this world's history, who in our baptism incorporates us as members of his risen body, who in the sacrament of Holy Communion binds us more closely to himself as those in and through whom he wills to carry on his work in the world—he is the same Jesus Christ who walked by the sea of Galilee, who bade his disciples love God with all their heart and mind and soul and strength, who prayed in agony in the Garden of Gethsemane, who stood before Caiaphas and Pontius Pilate and died on the cross of Calvary.

But what right have we, then, to call such an event as Christ's resurrection, equally with his death, a matter of history? The one, we feel, the death, was straightforward matter of fact, the kind of fact that historians are accustomed to deal with. The resurrection, even if our belief about it be true, was a different kind of fact, not the kind of fact that historians are accustomed to deal with.

We are tempted to reply that of course it is not the kind of fact that historians are *accustomed* to deal with, asking how what is *ex hypothesi* a unique occurrence can be any sort of a kind at all? But this slick verbal *riposte* evades the real question. The point at issue is not the uniqueness of the gospel story. It is the question whether for an adequate understanding of history we do not need to take into account factors which ordinarily historians are accustomed to ignore. I believe that Professor McIntyre is right in maintaining that this is the position we should take up.

To take it up does not mean that we are to be exempt from having regard to the generally accepted canons of historical study. We hold

3

that for a full understanding of historical events the materialist and humanist interpretations are inadequate; in our attempt to grasp what has occurred we have to read the evidence in relation to the creative and redemptive activity of God. The fact that these extra factors have to be taken into account does not justify any disregarding or twisting of the evidence in order to superimpose upon it the pattern of our faith. In a recent article in the *Journal of Theological Studies* Professor Nineham shows how the writing of history involves the confluence of two approaches, the *"a priori* argument about 'what *must* surely have happened' "*,* and the *a posteriori* argument from the empirical evidence concerning what did happen.[8] The historian who starts from the *a priori* end will be a bad historian if he is lacking in respect for the evidence provided by his *a posteriori* colleague. The aim of both must be a genuine reconciliation of their respective contributions.

Thus the Christian historian, who studies the empirical evidence in the light of the categories provided by his Christian faith, is doing what all historians do. The particular nature of his categories does not render his conclusions any more immune to historical criticism than are those of the materialist or humanist historian. St Luke wrote his gospel that Theophilus might know the certainty concerning the things wherein he was instructed. If the content of the Christian gospel is the proclamation of what God has done in the history of this world, we must be content with a revelation that has the kind of certainty that God has thought fit to give us.

Why should we ask for more? Here on earth, says St Paul, we walk by faith, not by sight. This is the certainty which is proper to faith, the certainty relevant to events in which time and eternity meet as the eternal Son of God enters upon and lives his human life and passes from his earthly ministry in space and time. It is the certainty proper to a faith which is no blind obscurantist faith that shuts its eyes to the march of historical studies but to a faith firmly grounded in a reasoned understanding of the nature of history and, indeed, of all human knowledge.

4

The particular problem I want to discuss in the light of what I have been saying is one of those arising from what is sometimes

8 April 1958, pp. 14-16.

called the eschatological element in the New Testament. But first a word or two about the use of this term. I hope I have said enough to make it clear that I have no sympathy with those who use the word "eschatological" as a smother word which will enable them to evade facing historical criticism, who speak of the whole earthly ministry of Christ as an "eschatological event" as though this lifted it above the plane of historicity. To speak of the coming of Christ as *the* "eschatological event" means, when we think it out, a combination of two things. It means (i) that we see in him the fulfilment of what the Jews were looking for as the *eschaton* of their hopes, and (ii) that as this fulfilment it involved the entry into the world's history of elements only explicable in terms of God's creative and redemptive activity, elements which, as we have seen, raise questions to which no human being can know the answer. In so far as we believe such elements actually to have entered into this world's history we can only justify our recognition of what occurred as being their embodiment by submitting them to the most rigorous scrutiny of historical research.

That being said, the particular question I want to discuss is what we are to make of the New Testament teaching about the end of the world. It will help me to make clear what I have to say if I relate it to Dr J. A. T. Robinson's book *Jesus and His Coming.*[9]

Dr Robinson's thesis, shorn of qualifications which he is too good a scholar to fail to make, may be summarized as follows. Our Lord did not himself predict that he would return on clouds of glory to final judgement either in the near future or at some more distant date. This is a doctrine which emerged during the New Testament period of church history and had been read back into our Lord's teaching by the time the gospels reached their present form. His own words about coming on clouds of glory referred to his vindication as Messiah, his coming to his throne at God's right hand. Dr Robinson marshalls evidence to show that the doctrine appears fully explicit in the later strata of original sources; those which reflect the minds of the earliest Christians are more in keeping with what Christ had actually predicted.

I want to suggest that the first thing we have to do is to disentangle and keep distinct the two questions: what our Lord actually taught and what the first Christians believed. I am not

[9] Dr Robinson was appointed Bishop of Woolwich in 1959.

denying what we have learned from the form critics, that the gospels are primarily evidence for what was being taught in the Church, and that we have to discover our Lord's own teaching through what they made of it. But I am sceptical of the assumption that the earlier the stratum the better the evidence either for what Christ taught or for what we ought to believe. Let me quote further from the passage in which I was criticizing the view that the primitive *kerygma* must be our standard for doctrinal teaching:

> If at the time of his preaching St. Peter was not able to see in the revelation all that St. Paul and St. John came to see, that does not mean that he was entrusted with a purer form of the doctrine, and that we get closer to the *depositum fidei* by ignoring their insights. What the Holy Spirit opened the eyes of St. Paul and St. John to see was part of the revelation itself, just as much as what was preached by St. Peter.

Moreover, it seems to me extremely doubtful whether there ever was formulated any such earlier doctrine as Dr Robinson suggests on p. 128 of his book where he writes:

> The question now is whether, prior to the introduction of 13. 26 Mark, or the community behind him, did not perhaps view the consummation of Jesus' work in closer accord with Jesus' own understanding of it. If it could be concluded that the Gospel as a whole was planned originally with that rather than the later conception as its climax, we should then have a much broader picture of the stage in the Church's thinking that lay behind the *Parousia* doctrine.

It is the attempt to trace a pattern of steady growth in the Church's thinking that seems to me doubtfully historical. There is no doubt that in the New Testament as we have it Dr Robinson's later doctrine is fully explicit. What had been one of the forms in which Jews looked for the first coming of Messiah has been postponed to be fulfilled in his return. I want to suggest the hypothesis that this was not the overlaying of an earlier by a later doctrine, but that there was no one earlier doctrine at all. The impression I get of the earlier Christians from the concluding chapters of the Gospels and the opening chapters of Acts is of a body of men who just did not know what to think. The Lord was risen and alive and among them. After the shock of the events of the previous few days this

staggering fact struck them dumbfounded. Somehow or other it was
true after all. He was the Messiah. They were "begotten again unto
a lively hope by the resurrection of Jesus Christ from the dead".
What form that "lively hope" was to take had still to be sorted out.
They were asking questions like "Lord, dost thou at this time restore
the kingdom to Israel?" There is nothing surprising in the fact
that they came to give substance to the "lively hope" by looking
to the future for the kind of coming of which they had been disappointed at the first advent of their Lord. There is no need to
postulate that this must have been a later belief which took the
place of an earlier. Nor need we think that unless there had been
such an earlier we have no ground for discarding the later. If the
result of a scholarly exegesis should be to show that the first
Christians, in bearing witness to their recognition of Jesus as
Messiah, pictured the fulfilment of his messiahship according to the
expectations that possessed their minds, this exegesis provides the
material for us to ask our question: what must the truth have
been and be if men who thought as they did put it like that?

We come to the question of our Lord himself, of what he thought
and taught. I am not going to call in question Dr Robinson's exegesis
here. It is a scholarly and judicious piece of work; for its discussion
in detail I must leave it to those better equipped than I am to
engage in its study on *a posteriori* lines. My part is to urge that such
study be set in the context of certain considerations that appear
to me to be of importance.

First, the trend of Gospel study in the last half century suggests
that we should be careful not to underrate the element of originality
in our Lord's thinking and teaching. Whether he thought of himself
as already Messiah, or as Messiah designate, it is surely clear that his
idea of messiahship did not correspond to any of those to be found
in existing schools of messianic expectation. By his contemporaries,
whose minds were conditioned by their notions of what Messiah
would be and do, he must often have been misunderstood, have
been thought to be saying something other than what he meant, and
this misunderstanding may have affected the form in which his
words were remembered and reported. With regard to his idea of
messiahship we have learned to beware of making the same mistake,
of thinking that we can explain his thought by quoting parallels to
show that he belonged to this or that contemporary school, or

derived his convictions from their source in this or that Old Testament passage. However much he may have found guidance and inspiration in the study of Holy Writ, and used the language of current thought, there can be no doubt that the revolution he wrought in the idea of messiahship, the revolution for which he was rejected as a blasphemous impostor and crucified, was his own. We must be prepared to find as much originality in his thought about the future destiny of Messiah as in that about his present vocation.

Secondly, I want to call attention to the significance of the inclusion of Simon the Zealot in the Twelve. It reminds us that apocalyptists were not the only school of thought in contemporary eschatology. Besides those who looked for the appearance of the Lord in the sky to bring to an end the present age with the advent of a new heaven and a new earth, there were those who looked for the raising up of an earthly ruler, a second David, who would rally God's people to arms, drive out the occupying power, establish the kingdom of God on earth and rule the nations of the world in God's name from its centre in the city which he had chosen to place his name there. We do not doubt that our Lord rejected this idea of his messianic destiny. We need not conclude that his only alternative was to accept that of the apocalyptists.

It may help us to grasp his situation if we reflect that to-day we are in similar case. On the one hand we have those who rest their hopes for the future on the possibility of human progress. They look for the coming of an earthly paradise to be achieved by increasing scientific control of the forces of nature and the spread of education. Their methods may be different from those advocated by the zealots, but their goal is essentially the same. On the other hand are those who despair of this world's future, who think of it as destined to be burnt up in the ever-lasting bonfire and pin their hopes on their expectation of the return of Christ in glory to judgement.

The zealots of our Lord's time differed from the humanists of to-day in that they believed in God, that their leader and his followers would be raised up and inspired from on high and fight and rule as the armies of the living God. Granted this difference, I have shown in my book on the Atonement that both kinds of expectation, both that which looks for the fulfilment of God's creative purpose in the history of this world and that which despairs of this world's perfection and looks for its catastrophic destruction, are to be found in the New Testament. Would this be so if the Lord had been known unmistakably to have committed himself to one or the other?

Further, let me quote my comments on sayings in which he is reported to have used the language of apocalyptic:

> It is now generally agreed that in matters of science and history, on questions of empirical fact, our Lord during His earthly ministry, in His incarnate human mind, shared with His contemporaries in their knowledge. We find no difficulty in holding that so far as the details of past history are concerned He accepted what was commonly believed among His people at the time. I cannot see why we should adopt a different principle when what we are concerned with are the details of future history. There is ample evidence that the apocolyptic imagery He used was that which He took over from current Jewish thought in the same way as, no doubt, He took over the account of the creation of the world in six days. We have learned that we can hold fast to the truth of the world's creation by God and man's responsibility to his Creator while substituting for that account our evolutionary view of its historical origin. There is no disloyalty to our Lord in accepting on His authority the certainty of divine judgement while preserving an open mind on the question of the historical process whereby in the future the rescue of God's creation from its infection by evil shall be consummated.[10]

I have twice spoken of questions to which no human beings know the answers. If there be such a class, it must surely include some of those concerning the relation of time to eternity. No one since Kant can ignore the paradox of the impossibility of conceiving time and space either as limited or as without limits. We arrive at what is not the same but a similar impasse when we try to imagine what can conceivably be the *eschaton* and *telos* of this world's history, the fulfilment of God's creative and redemptive purpose for this world in space and time. I submit that we have no right to demand that we shall find in the teaching of Christ an answer to such questions, that to do so is to prescribe to God the kind of revelation we think he should have provided instead of being content to accept that which he has thought fit to give us.

My approach, you will have noticed, has been of the kind which Professor Nineham has called *a priori*. I leave it to you, who have to

[10] *The Doctrine of the Atonement*, p. 126.

follow the *a posteriori* road in order to satisfy your examiners' just demand for exact scholarship, to investigate whether the evidence will support my reading of it. According to that reading Jesus found himself surrounded by differing messianic and eschatological expectations in which men thought to picture to themselves the shape of things to come, the actual course of future events in history. He was too wise to identify himself with any prediction which should profess to give in advance the kind of information about questions of empirical fact for which men on earth must be content to wait and see. We shall not be cured of our theological schizophrenia until we cease from the delusion that somewhere within the pages of the Bible we must be able to find the kind of answers to questions which he was unwilling to give.

2

THE INSPIRATION OF THE BIBLE [1]

C. F. EVANS

2 Cor. 4. 7 : But we have this treasure in earthen vessels, that the exceeding greatness of the power may be of God, and not from ourselves.

THE POSITION of a Faculty of Theology in a university is not without ambiguity. On the one hand, it stands alongside the other Faculties, pursuing the argument where it goes, by the application of those methods which are proper to its subject. If it remains true to the best traditions of its past, it need not fear the accusation of unprofessional conduct. For it was the theologians who did more than any to bring into being those methods of literary and historical analysis which now govern, not only their own studies, but the studies of others also. So far from its being the case, as is commonly supposed, that the modern methods of historical investigation were first perfected outside the field of theological studies, and were then applied, perhaps somewhat reluctantly, to the study of the Bible and Christian history, the opposite is near the truth. The pioneers in the field of textual criticism, Richard Bentley and Carl Lachmann, graduated in their science not only on classical texts but on the text of the New Testament, and, perhaps significantly, Bentley never produced his text because he found the conditions so much more complex in the study of the New Testament than in the study of classical texts. When Wilamowitz dedicated his Homeric Studies to the Old Testament scholar Julius Wellhausen he greeted him as the pioneer of that method of rolling back the history of the transmission of the text which he himself was now using. Methods evolved within the heart of Christian studies, in order to enable

[1] Reprinted from *Theology*, Vol. LIX, No. 427 (Jan. 1956), pp. 11-17.

theologians to handle the problems presented by their own subject matter, have contributed greatly to the specifically modern study of history in general. The theologian wishes therefore to stand as a scholar alongside other scholars.

On the other hand, he cannot remain unaware of the implications which his studies have for others. This is the case with other scholars also, including, of late, the scientists, but with the biblical scholar it is especially so. He cannot forget that the subject matter of his study is that through which, to many thousands in actuality, and to all men potentially, the living God speaks his living word; or that his subject hardly has a right to exist, and certainly would not exist, except as the handmaid of the Church. He reminds himself that the Lord did not walk and talk in Galilee in order that learned journals might be published. He cannot remain unmoved by the feeling expressed by P. T. Forsyth when he wrote: "I do not believe in verbal inspiration. I am with the critics in principle. But the true minister ought to find the words and phrases of the Bible so full of spiritual food and felicity that he has some difficulty in not believing in verbal inspiration." There is a tension between his critical method and his subject matter, when that subject matter is placed in its fullest context, between the analytic and often negative approach of the one, and the unitive, affirmative nature of the other. How acute this tension can become appears from the recent controversial letters in *The Times* newspaper, since published as a pamphlet, on Fundamentalism, and although the controversy arose over events that were to take place in Cambridge, the problem is very much with us here too in Oxford, and is not unconnected with claims to a widespread religious revival. No doubt fundamentalism has its sociological and psychological aspects, according to which it is part of a search for security in a world terrifyingly insecure. Those also who know the human heart will not deny that criticism at times has been made a smoke screen for much wilful rebellion and culpable unbelief. But the problem goes much deeper than that, and anyone concerned with Christian truth is in some measure involved in it. From time to time the biblical scholar, however humble his place, must take his eyes off his immediate work and look at the larger scene.

The inspiration of the Scriptures is not a dogma. At least the Church as a whole has never ventured a dogmatic definition of it.

The experience of the Church in those periods when one single view has predominated—allegorism in the fourth century or biblicism in the nineteenth—is not such as to encourage us to look for such a definition. When the Church has been most vigorous she has assumed the Bible to be inspired, and has got on with the business of interpreting it. Inspiration is a mystery; like all divine mysteries it is hidden from our sight. But the results and impress of inspiration are matters subject to our observation, and we have the right to expect that, by observing them carefully, we may catch some glimpse of how the divine spirit operates, and intends to operate, towards and in our human nature, as Moses was permitted to catch some glimpse of God's hinder parts as he passed by. Indeed, must we not go further or perish? Must we not claim that the same Holy Spirit, who spake by the prophets, and who inspired the Scriptures, does, in another and lesser mode of his operation, lead men to a right critical exercise of the natural reason upon the same Scriptures? It was the absence of any such suggestion in the letters to *The Times*, with one exception, that was perhaps the most disturbing feature about them. When Charles Gore wrote his essay on "The Holy Spirit and Inspiration" in *Lux Mundi* he delivered many in one section of the Church of England, and possibly others also, from the alternatives of obscurantism or unbelief; and it was part of the strength of that essay that he refused to treat the question of inspiration until he had first written at length about the Holy Spirit. He noted as the marks of his working that it was gradual, having as its object the consecration of the whole of nature, that it was varied, employing manifold expressions of the natural genius, and that it was social, bringing men to the height of their individuality within a holy community. Sixty-five years have passed since he wrote, but if much has happened in biblical studies the issues remain much the same. The objections now are not markedly different from those of Liddon when he complained of Gore's restrictions upon the predictive power of prophecy, his alliance with rationalistic theories of composition, his extension of the dramatic hypothesis to writings which seemed to claim an historical character, and the admission of myth as a constituent element in the Old Testament. And if there is much now of which Gore would have disapproved, it would not be difficult to show that it is in line with principles which he himself laid down as to the substance, the instruments and the locus of divine revelation.

First, as to its substance. Out of what does God make his revelation to us? The more thoroughly historical investigation is applied the more it removes old landmarks and brings to light the intimate connection between the Scriptures on the one hand, and the concepts and practices, the myth and ritual, of the total environment in which Israel and the Christian Church at any time lived on the other. One by one characteristics which had been thought to be peculiar to the religion of the Bible are paralleled, and are no longer *differentia* of that religion from the general run of semitic belief or hellenistic mysticism. Nor can these similarities be limited to certain periods labelled primitive, and therefore easily detached and left on one side; they pervade throughout, as each new stage in the development takes something from the old. There is no naked biblical religion, but only that which comes to us clothed in the thought forms and culture of its age. Even if we say, as we must, that the Scriptures lie under the impress of the prophets, and that the Spirit spake by the prophets, this does not mean that the prophets were altogether peculiar. Rather does it seem to mean that through the prophets history is distinguished from nature as the principal medium of God's revelation, is made pre-eminent over it and interpretative of it. The identification of nature with deity is broken. Its processes of sowing and harvest, begetting and fatherhood, are set free from the cycle of nature so that they can be made to point to a creative work of God, a kingly rule and judgement of God, who makes himself known in his particular acts, and as he encounters men in their history. In doing so the prophets initiated a faith that was progressive. They opened the way to a real future, and made of religion something which looked forward and pressed onwards to further embodiment and incarnation. This embodiment is found only partly in the Judaism to which their prophecy gave rise; it is found fully in Christ. But Christ himself is so completely clothed with our natural life, and is so closely united with that Jewish form of it which prophets and rabbis had created out of it, that for that very reason he can become a scandal when finality is claimed for him. Though he be God's final revelation to us, yet his identification with us is such that he does not bring things to a stop; rather he opens up an even wider future for the world, which is now a future in Christ, and its goal the summing up of all things in him.

It would seem, therefore, that the mode of God's revelation which the Scriptures themselves suggest, the more stringently they are examined, is represented neither by a doctrine of immanence, in which nature is left where it was, identified with deity, nor by a doctrine of transcendence in which nature is left on one side, and God brings something new and strange down on our heads like a ton of bricks, but rather by what St John Chrysostom called the *sunkatabasis* of God, the condescension of God to the measure of his creation, by which he moulds it from within to be an expression of his will. The great texts of St John and St Paul, "The Word became flesh" and Christ "took upon himself the form of a servant" speak to us not only of the Incarnation itself, but of the way God at all times has been dealing with men. If this then is the way that God reveals himself, this is the way in which we must receive his revelation, with due respect for the means through which it is made. It thus becomes less possible for us than for our predecessors to cut the Scriptures up into that which is credible to a twentieth-century man and that which can be left behind as old clothes. A deeper analysis gives them back to us more as an organic whole; but, once the facts are scientifically known, this can be on one condition only, namely, that we admit those things which Liddon denied, and admit them to a far greater extent than Gore dreamt of asking, viz. rationalistic theories of composition, the extension of the dramatic hypothesis to writings which claim a historical character, and the presence of myth as a constituent element in the Scriptures.

Secondly, as to the instruments. It is common at the present time to stress that the Christian revelation is a revelation through history. This is entirely proper, and as a corrective to a scholasticism, Catholic or Protestant, which supposes the Bible to be a repository of divine propositions, very salutary. But of itself it is not sufficient. The best history in the Bible, as we understand history, is to be found in the first book of Maccabees, but it would be a hardy theologian who would contend that the core of the revelation was to be found in that book. If we were looking for it during this period we would be more likely to find it in the contemporary book of Daniel, not by reason of the history contained in that book, which is dubious indeed, but by reason of certain great conceptions and images, the eternal kingdom of God, the saints of the most high, the Son of Man upon the clouds, by means of which the history is interpreted. Event and language belong together in the Scriptures as matter and form in the sacrament, the latter giving life to the former. But of what kind is this language? Older writers used to speak of the Scriptures as the language of the Holy Ghost, and old-fashioned lexicons were in the habit of listing the words peculiar to the Bible under the heading of "biblical Greek". But, lecturing in 1863, J. B. Lightfoot let drop the remark that if we could only re-cover the letters which ordinary people wrote without any thought of being literary we should have the greatest possible help in under-standing the language of the New Testament. What Lightfoot desiderated has come to pass. Egyptian waste-paper baskets have yielded up sufficient of their contents to show that the language of the Scriptures is none other than the vernacular tongue. One by one instances of biblical Greek are struck off the list. There is, in this sense, no language specially minted for the conveyance of divine truth. But further knowledge of the facts does not destroy what Schleiermacher called "the capacity of Christianity to mould language"; it only locates it elsewhere. For the more closely the language of the Scriptures is scrutinized the more it appears that the language understanded of the people undergoes in the Scriptures a subtle deflection from its ordinary meaning, sometimes even as far as the opposite of its ordinary meaning, and it is difficult to resist the conclusion that this is the result of the pressure upon men's minds and hearts of their relation to God, and of his revelation of himself to them. Covenant, kingship, war and peace, salvation and judgement, shepherd and sheep, marriage and adultery, these words, which govern men's thoughts and desires, are taken out of the sphere of men's natural and worldly occupations, are redirected in such a way that they can no longer be exhausted by a purely natural content, and become symbols of that supernatural life which God desires to give to men in communion with himself. With these images Christ, whose life and work falls so completely within the natural, clothes himself, uniting them and refashioning them so that they are no longer disparate or contradictory. In their fullest supernatural meaning they fit him alone. But if through the Spirit's work this language is no longer the language of primitive natural science which it once was, neither has it become the language of discursive reasoning fitted to philosophy and systematic theology. It is rather the language of poetry, and none the less poetry because its craftsmanship is largely unconscious and its object not the poet's wonder and delight in the creature, but the praise of, and obedience to, the Creator. Perhaps the theologian has been too easily scared away from the poet, whom Coventry Patmore once described as "holding a strange position in the hierarchy of things halfway between the saint and Balaam's ass". It will not do, therefore, simply to reiterate "the Bible says". We are concerned with what God is saying, and with the way in which he says it. Fundamentalism ignores this, and brings to the interpretation of the language of the Bible a literalness and hardness which, it must be noted, is of very recent origin, because it is the product of an age that has come to assume that there is only one kind of truth and only one kind of vehicle of truth. "Fundamentalism", wrote Michael Roberts, "may have the Bible for its mother, but it has for its father Thomas Hobbes . . . who regarded poetry as trivial, and who denied that there were any things which needed to be said which could only be said through the poetic use of language." Hence, he continued, "when the modern atheist denies that he has a Father in heaven he is denying something which his ancestors never asserted, for he is interpreting in the strictest terms of physical time and space and matter words which were first used with no thought of such interpretation".

Thirdly, as to the locus of revelation. The critical analysis of the Scriptures, as it pressed further and deeper, leads at every point— and this is a truth still unwelcome to some—to the Church, to the people of God, as the sphere within which the language of revelation has worked, and continues to work, with power for the drawing of the natural life of men into a living touch with the supernatural life of God. The Gospels, it is now seen, are not biographies, but compositions, more poetically subtle than was imagined, out of stories and traditions which already had a history behind them in the faith and worship of the Church, out of which they came, and which they existed to serve. And, as the Fourth Gospel reminds us, the events, and the faith and life to which the events gave rise, are so smelted that the one cannot be had without the other. In epistles, in which apostolic men address the Church, we stumble at any moment upon fragments of creed, catechism, or liturgy, and there are few passages which can be fully understood except within the Church's life. It would seem to be part of the mystery of inspiration that so much of what has become for us Holy Scripture was domestic to the Church, and almost occasional in its origin. God's way of admitting us into his revelation, it would appear, is to allow us to overhear snatches of his conversation with the Church, and so to draw us into its tradition and life. It is not enough for Bible societies to publish the figures of Bibles distributed throughout the world as though in themselves they were a matter for simple congratulation. The Scriptures are not alive except within the society which they were intended to create and recreate. It is not the public but the private use of them which stands in need of justification.

As Christians we ought to desire to live under the authority of God, and under the authority of persons or things only as they minister to us the authority of God. It is possible so to glorify God's instruments as to detract from the supremacy of the God whose instruments they are. The desire for an infallibility short of the infallibility of God, be it of Church or Bible, is an idolatrous lust. And we must beware even of how we think of the infallibility of God himself. For all arguments for infallibility are *a priori*, and divine infallibility is generally held to be a plain inference from God's nature. "If God is God then surely he does this"; "if God is God then it follows that he will have done that". That is how the argument runs. And the questions that the critic is bound to ask are: "does he?" and "has he?", and asking them he appeals to the evidence. The critic has no right to dictate to men what they shall believe; his task is much humbler than that. He is a mere hewer of wood and drawer of water. But he has the right to ask that men take his work into account, if it is truly done, in making up their minds what to believe. And if his work is chiefly a preoccupation with the earthenness of those vessels which it has pleased God to use, it need not for that reason be only a negative or destructive work, for it can prepare the way at any moment for the acknowledgement that the exceeding greatness of the power is of God and not from ourselves.

3

BIBLE AND DOGMA [1]

J. BURNABY

THE question we are to consider is this: What is the nature of the connection between the canonical Scriptures and the dogmas of the Christian Church, the statements in which the essential elements of our faith are formulated? In what sense do we or can we claim that Christian doctrine as we may present it to-day is derived from Scripture or founded upon it, and by what method is the derivation or foundation established?

We may conveniently begin by reminding ourselves of the terms in which this question was answered by the English Reformers in the Thirty-nine Articles of Religion, "agreed upon by the Archbishops and Bishops of both Provinces and the whole Clergy, in the Convocation holden at London in the year 1562 for the avoiding of diversities of opinions and for the establishing of consent touching true religion."

"Holy Scripture containeth all things necessary to salvation: so that whatsoever is not read therein, nor may be proved thereby, is not to be required of any man that it should be believed as an Article of the Faith, or be thought requisite or necessary to salvation." (Art. VI.)

"The three Creeds, Nicene Creed, Athanasius's Creed, and that which is commonly called the Apostles' Creed, ought thoroughly to be received and believed; for they may be proved by most certain warrants of Holy Scripture." (Art. VIII.)

"The Church, as it ought not to decree anything against Holy

[1] Reprinted from the *Church Quarterly Review*, Vol. CLIX, No. 331 (April-June, 1958), pp. 179-92.

Writ, so besides the same ought it not to enforce anything to be believed for necessity of salvation." (Art. XX.)

What the framers of the Articles call beliefs "necessary to salvation" are those which I have rather more cautiously described as "essential elements" of the Christian faith. The purpose of the Reformers was to release these essential doctrines from the accretions or perversions in which the Catholic Church of the Middle Ages was thought to have involved them; and for this purpose all that was needed to be asked was whether a doctrine was contained in Scripture or could be proved thereby. They would doubtless have been prepared to indicate those "certain warrants" of Holy Scripture which "proved" the statements of the Athanasian Creed : e.g. those which assert that Christ is one, "not by confusion of substance but by unity of person"; or that in the Trinity "none is afore or after other, none is greater or less than another; but the whole three Persons are co-eternal together and co-equal"— and so to justify the Creed's further statement : "He therefore that will be saved must thus think of the Trinity." But it was by no means so easy for the Reformers to give plausibility to their view of the relation of doctrine to Scripture as it was for their Catholic opponents to maintain their own. Both sides took for granted the finality of the Christian revelation : Catholic no more than Protestant would allow that anything has been or could be added to that revelation since the death of the last Apostle. But it was and remains Roman doctrine, not only that unwritten tradition received by the Church from the Apostles is a source of Christian dogma equally valid with the letter of Scripture, but that the Church has been empowered by the Holy Spirit to clarify what was obscure and draw out what was implicit in Scripture itself. And a doctrine which cannot be found in Scripture, and may be difficult to prove by any "certain warrants" of Scripture, can much more easily be defended as making clear or explicit what was in Scripture contained only obscurely or by implication.

In the controversies of the sixteenth century, however, there were other presuppositions, with regard both to the inspiration of Scripture and to the nature of the revelation contained in it, which were common to both sides. It was not doubted either that the revelation of God had been given in the form of statements having absolute truth, or that the Scripture in which this revelation is conveyed was exempt from error in every particular. It followed, first, that the truth of a doctrine expressly stated in Scripture is thereby guaranteed; and second, that doctrines not expressly stated in Scripture may be "proved", if they are deducible from Scriptural texts used as premises. It must also follow, that if any two statements in Scripture appear to conflict with one another, it must be possible to show that the conflict is only apparent; for the truth of both is equally guaranteed by that inspiration.

These are consequences of the particular beliefs about the inspiration of Scripture and the method of revelation which were held in the sixteenth century. In our own time different views on both these subjects have become fairly common ground among Christian theologians. It is now widely held that the revelation of which Scripture is the record is not to be identified with a number of statements about God—though it may and indeed must lead those who accept it to make such statements. The Scriptural revelation is the act of God making himself known to men as Person to persons—as Creator, Lord, and Father to creatures, servants, and children—and by the same act reconciling the world to himself. God has come in Jesus Christ to meet men; and the New Testament is the witness of men who have encountered Christ and have found in that encounter the knowledge of God. That which they have seen and heard they declare unto us also, that we also may have fellowship with them; and their fellowship is with the Father and with his Son Jesus Christ. The personal knowledge on which such fellowship is grounded cannot be conveyed in statements any more than I can make you know my friend by telling you about him. The purpose of the statements made by those who have seen and heard is to enable those who have not to receive the same revelation and enter into the same fellowship; but the statements themselves are not and cannot be the revelation. And this is borne out by the unmistakeable fact that the writers of the New Testament (like those of the Old) have different ways of expressing their witness to the revelation. St Paul, St John, and the *auctor ad Hebraeos* are speaking about the same thing; but they speak differently, and the differences are not to be eliminated or reduced. Their inspiration has not flattened out their individualities or their idiosyncrasies; it is to be discerned, not in identity or even in consistency of verbal statement, but in the response which they have been enabled to make to the Word of God in Christ, and in the power given them to communicate that Word to others.

Accordingly, the student of the New Testament will not approach his inquiry from the viewpoint of what he has learnt to regard as orthodox Christian doctrine. He will not be searching the literature of the primitive Church for pieces which can be assembled so as to compose a doctrinal system as nearly as possible identifiable with the later orthodoxy. Instead of this, he will allow each New Testament writing to speak for itself: he will assume neither that all the writers must agree with one another, nor that the same writer must always be consistent with himself; he will take seriously St Paul's claim to have become all things to all men, and its natural implication of readiness to adapt forms of statement to the situation of the persons addressed; and he will thus be prepared to find that the New Testament contains not one uniform theology but a variety of theological types.

We are accustomed to read the sermons in the early chapters of Acts as preserving for us the general tenor of the Gospel as the Apostles first presented it to their own countrymen. That Jesus, whom God had raised from the dead, was the expected Messiah, the pre-destined instrument of salvation, that in his coming God had visited and redeemed his people as he had promised to their forefathers, that forgiveness of sins and the power of the Holy Spirit were available to all who would through the baptism of repentance take Jesus for their Lord, and wait in confidence for the final manifestation of God's Kingdom on earth—this was the substance of the *kerygma*, the proclamation of the good news of Christ; and to accept it was to have a place in the true Israel, to inherit the sure promises of God.

Obviously, a mission preaching in such terms would be intelligible only to Jews or to those who had become more or less familiar with the Jewish religion—the "God-fearing" fringe of the Synagogue in the Roman Empire. Acts makes it clear that in fact the Christian mission began everywhere in the synagogue; and most of the infant churches must have looked more like non-conforming offshoots of the local synagogue than anything else. Acts offers us only a single specimen of a missionary address to an exclusively heathen audience; but it is not likely that St Paul's unsuccessful experiment at Athens represents a typical method of approach where no Jewish background could be assumed. We know very little of how the Gospel might be preached when the missionaries "turned to the Gentiles": in all probability the local church continued to grow generally by poaching on the synagogue—to the very understandable indignation of the latter. But whether the convert was well or ill informed on the faith of Judaism, and whatever it may have been in the Christian preaching that carried conviction to his mind, when once he had accepted the Gospel and entered into the fellowship of the Christian community, the *Ecclesia* of the Messiah, he would go on to receive in that fellowship what Acts calls the doctrine of the Apostles, the *didache*, the teaching which is exemplified for us in the New Testament Epistles and the tradition preserved for us in the Gospels of all that Jesus himself began to do and to *teach*.

The last verses of St Matthew's Gospel record the risen Christ's charge to his Apostles to go and make disciples of all nations, *teaching* them to observe all things that he had commanded them; and there is no reason to doubt that this fairly represents what the Apostles did in fact teach their first converts, and that it was in this way that the memory of Christ's own teaching was preserved. It is probable also that from the first the Scriptures were constantly searched for confirmation of the claim made in the *kerygma* that Jesus was indeed the Christ foretold in them. In particular, the story of the Passion was so told as to show that even in the rejection of Christ by his own people the Scriptures had been fulfilled.

So far, there would be nothing to give rise to serious divergences. Teachers were a gift of God to the Church, no less than Apostles and Prophets (1 Cor. 12. 28). But the teaching itself, at least as soon as it came to be given in a number of more or less isolated groups of converts, would vary both in form and content with the varying personalities and experiences of the individual teachers. No doubt, it was variation of this kind that gave rise to the so-called "parties" in the Corinthian Church which St Paul deplores: "I am of Paul, I of Apollos, I of Cephas." Even in the case of the Synoptic Gospels, we have to come to appreciate the different lights in which a common tradition of the Church appears as presented by a number of different compilers. St Paul himself can speak of a *typos didaches*, a pattern of teaching, to which the Christians of Rome have been "delivered"—entrusted as to a guardian; yet the pattern of his

own teaching in Romans and Galatians is not the same as in
2 Corinthians or in Colossians/Ephesians.

But the individuality of the teacher is not the only or the most
important source of variety in the teaching. It was not long, as we
know, before questions of truth and error arose. The first and most
momentous controversy bore upon the terms of admission to the
Church for Gentile converts; and it was out of this controversy that
the characteristically Pauline doctrines of grace, faith, and justification, set forth in Galatians and Romans, emerged. And as soon as
churches had been established in centres of Hellenistic culture such
as Corinth we find St Paul involved in fresh controversies, compelling him to defend the Gospel he had preached by further
elaborations of his own understanding of it, ending in the "high
Christology" of the Epistle to the Colossians. In the Johannine
writings, the effect of polemical impulse upon theological development, though not always so apparent on the surface, is not less
determinative. "John" is confronting danger to the faith on two
sides: it has to be defended and asserted both against dissipation
into the false spiritualism of Greek religious thought, and against
imprisonment in an unspiritual Jewish eschatology. And these needs
evoke the characteristically Johannine doctrines of the Word made
flesh and of the present possession of eternal life.

If this is anything like a true account of what we find in the
New Testament, if we cannot speak of any one homogeneous
theological pattern to which all its writers conform, it becomes all
the more difficult to avoid the question, How did that pattern which
we call orthodoxy come to shape itself during the four centuries
that followed?

So far, we have not distinguished "doctrine" from "dogma"; and
we are accustomed to-day to speak of Christian doctrine as though
it meant the body or sum of accepted dogmas of the faith. But it
would clearly be inappropriate to use the word "dogma" of the
didache, the teaching or instruction in the faith which in the
New Testament, as we have seen, is to be distinguished from
the *kerygma*, the central message of the Gospel as delivered by its
missionaries. Doctrine, in general, is the form which Christian
teaching assumes in the hands of an individual teacher or group
of teachers. A particular doctrine will be the expression given in
such a context to a particular element of the faith which is the

subject of instruction—whether it be the person of Christ, the significance of his death, the nature of the Church, or the principles of Christian life and conduct. Dogma, in the strict sense of the word, is a decision taken by competent authority in order to settle a dispute about doctrine; and in this sense perhaps the only dogma contained in the New Testament is the decision by the Apostolic Council of Jerusalem (in Acts 15) that circumcision should not be enforced upon Gentile converts—which was what certain men who had come down from Judaea, had *taught* the brethren at Antioch. The great age of dogma is of course the century and a half which followed the adoption of Christianity as the religion of the Empire, when diversity of teaching was regarded as damaging to the effectiveness of that religion as a bond of unity in the State. Dogmatic orthodoxy became the postulate of an established Church.

But the foundations of dogma were being laid in the development of doctrine which is traceable from the beginning.

In the second century, the defenders of Catholic Christianity against the menace of Gnosticism were accustomed to appeal to a *Regula Fidei*, a Rule of Faith, by which the identity and continuity of Christian teaching was ensured. This Rule, as it is quoted e.g. by Irenaeus and Tertullian, shows no verbal fixity; but it runs closely parallel to the baptismal confession of faith, which was already becoming stereotyped in the form of what we know as the Old Roman Creed—of which our Apostles' Creed is the direct descendant. There is sufficient evidence from the second century that the candidate for baptism was required to affirm his adherence to the faith, by answering *Credo*, "I believe", to a series of questions corresponding to the three sections of the *Regula*. The structure of the confessions is naturally framed upon the formula of baptism in the Three-fold Name, which is at least as old as St Matthew's Gospel; and its content is entirely biblical. The New Testament seems to reflect a period when baptism had no preliminary conditions beyond acceptance of the invitation extended in the *kerygma*. Only the Western text of Acts 8. 37, in the account of the baptism of the Ethiopian eunuch, shows the beginnings of a formal baptismal confession: "I believe that Jesus Christ is the Son of God." On the other hand, the New Testament preserves certain formulae of Christian confession, of which the most concise is the "Jesus is Lord" of Romans 10. 9 and 1 Corinthians 12. 3. For the Jewish convert, acceptance of the Gospel would imply acceptance of the claim that Jesus (in the words of Romans 1. 4) has been "designated Son of God with power in the Holy Spirit by the resurrection from the dead". For the Gentile, the confession that Jesus is Lord would need to be set upon its Jewish background of faith in the One Creator and the working of his Spirit in man. No doubt, in such confessions, dogma is already present in a rudimentary form; and the process of expansion into the *Regula Fidei* would be natural enough. But what we have to observe is that the second-century *Regula*, and even the later Apostles' Creed, exhibits so much *less* development in doctrine than is to be found within the New Testament itself. The Christ-ology of the Apostles' Creed is limited to the titles Son of God and Lord, the Virgin Birth, the Resurrection and Ascension, and the future coming as Judge; and *all* this (except the Virgin Birth) is present in the sermons of Peter in Acts 2 and 10.

As a summary of Christian doctrine, the *Regula*, even in comparison with the primitive *kerygma*, has an extremely jejune appearance. But of course doctrine, teaching, is just what it is not. In the second century as in the first, teaching, instruction in the faith, is something that follows upon conversion—with the difference that whereas in the beginning it was given to persons already admitted by baptism to full membership of the Christian community, it later takes on the character of a preparation for baptism. We know very little of the early history of the cate-chumenate; but we can safely assume that when the baptismal ceremony has come to include a questioning of the candidate in terms of the *Regula Fidei*, the candidate will not have been expected to reply to such questioning without *some* previous instruction in the meaning and implications of the profession he was to make. As to the nature of this instruction we have no clear evidence till much later : the earliest surviving examples of Catechetical Lectures are those given by Cyril of Jerusalem in the middle of the fourth century, which (in Dr Telfer's judgement) bring to us in spite of their date the "voice of the ante-Nicene Church". By that time, the general pattern of preparation for baptism has become well established—a course of instruction during Lent, leading up to the *Traditio Symboli*, the "delivery" by bishop to catechumens of the Creed which they are to profess. The instruction itself was the bishop's responsibility, and we can estimate the freedom with which it was exercised by comparing, e.g., the *Catecheses* of Cyril with the *De Fide et Symbolo* of Augustine a generation later. There must have been wide variations in the doctrinal "type" affected by bishops in different churches.

But it is not here that we shall find the source of dogmatic development; though the *Catechesis* is likely to show the effects of such developments as have occurred. The formulation of Catholic doctrine which went on from the second century to the fifth was a process evoked by two needs: first, the need to defend Christianity against hostile misrepresentation and commend it to the more thoughtful elements of pagan society; and second, the need to maintain the distinctive character of the faith against the disintegrating effects of divergent teaching within the Church. We can compare, in the New Testament, the needs which exercise the writers of Acts on the one hand, and of the Pastoral Epistles on the other. In the second century, the *Logos*-doctrine of the Apologists represents the Church's endeavour to conciliate and attract the educated heathen: the polemic against Gnostic dualism represents the Church's refusal to tear up its own roots in Hebrew religion.

In the third century, we find in the school of Alexandria a modification both of the positive and of the negative reaction of Christian teaching to Greek thought: the *Logos*-doctrine becomes more Christian, and Christianity less anti-Gnostic. And nearly all the great doctrinal controversies of the fourth and fifth centuries issue from the intellectual legacy of the great Alexandrians. In this legacy the most dangerous element was the system of biblical exegesis with which Origen had buttressed his vast and precarious structure of Christian-Gnostic philosophy and Christian-Gnostic spirituality. It is often said that Alexandrian allegorism saved the Old Testament for the Christian Church; but the price was high, for it came perilously near to treating the New Testament, and especially the Gospels, in a fashion that must have cut Christianity loose from its moorings in history. It proved the doctrines it upheld by "certain warrants" of Holy Scripture only by dint of imposing on the proof-texts the meaning required in order that they might warrant the doctrine.

Unfortunately, the method of reading into Holy Scripture whatever one wishes to be able to read out of it did not come to an end with the disuse of allegorism; and it still presents a temptation to the dogmatist which is not easily resistible. There is only one way of receiving from Scripture the truth which it has been given to convey, and that is to let the texts speak to us in their own language—learning all we can about that language from those best qualified to instruct us; for we must train our ear so that it may hear what the Spirit said unto the churches of the first century. The reverence with which we should approach the New Testament is the scientist's reverence for the facts which he seeks to understand. Its authority for us is the authority of fact, and the fact is simply that when Christ came this was how men were led (as we believe, *non sine Deo*) to speak of what his coming meant to them. What gives to the writings of the New Testament their *unique* authority, an authority by which all later doctrine must consent to be controlled, is their character as the original documents of a religion that claims to rest upon historical events. "No man cometh unto the Father but by me", said Christ. We have to accept a situation in which none of us can come to Christ but by the witness of his Apostles; and our nearest echo of that witness is in the New Testament.

It might of course be maintained that it should be the work of Christian teachers in every generation, first, to understand the Scriptures, to distinguish what gives unity to the message of the Bible from what is peculiar to this or that writer, what is central from what is peripheral, what is essential from what is accidental; and then, on the basis of such understanding, to develop a doctrine of the act of God in Christ which will be intelligible, or at least not meaningless, to the contemporary mind. But as we know, this is not what has happened. Suppose we take the *Regula Fidei* of the second century, or the Apostles' Creed, as giving us the essential structure of Christian belief. Then we must recognize that the Church has not been content with it. The Church, in certain critical situations of its history, superimposed upon that Rule or Creed statements about matters quite beyond human ascertainment or comprehension: not only about the way in which it has pleased God to become man, but about the eternal being of God himself. And the Church did so, because such statements seemed *at the time* to be necessary in order to maintain the unity and fidelity of Christian teaching. The bishops who took part in the decisions of the first four Ecumenical Councils were not consciously legislating for the Church of a thousand, two thousand, or twenty thousand years later in time than their own: they were thinking of the Church for which they were responsible, of the faith and salvation of their own flocks. But their decisions have in fact become dogmas of the Christian religion, with an authority to all appearances as permanent and inescapable as that of the New Testament itself. We can imagine that Christian *teaching* might use different language about God from that in which the Fathers framed the dogma of the Trinity; but we cannot imagine that any teaching which did not *mean* that God has truly revealed himself as Father, Son, and Holy Ghost could ever win recognition as Christian.

Let us then take this as an essential Christian belief, and try to see how it can be said to belong to the faith of the New Testament. We may fairly claim that the confession "Jesus is Lord" is central to that faith, common to every *typos didaches,* every variety of doctrine that is to be found in Epistle, Gospel, or Apocalypse. Nor can it be disputed that every writer of the New Testament believes himself to speak from within the faith of the Old, to be an Israelite indeed. For the Greek-speaking Jew, *Kyrios,* Lord, was the holy Name of God: his daily profession of faith was, "Hear, O Israel. the Lord thy God is *one Lord*". Evidently, *Kyrios Iesous* did not and could not mean for the Christian convert a sheer identification of Jesus with Jehovah; but neither did it or could it mean the ascription to Jesus of a Lordship independent or secondary. What it did mean was that the man whom Pilate had crucified and whom God had raised from the dead was the object of *worship,* of a religious devotion not different in kind from the reverence and trust rendered by a devout Israelite to the God of his fathers. The astonishing thing is that no New Testament writer appears to feel that his devotion to Christ involves any disloyalty to the one God, any setting up of Lord against Lord: there is no hint of competition or rivalry between the Lord Jesus and the Lord Jehovah. The Lord God is still *one* Lord. Jesus is not Jehovah, but the Lordship ascribed to him is none other than the unique Lordship of the God of Israel. In Jesus the one God is revealing himself as Lord and Saviour: **Jesus bears the authority of God.**

What has made it possible for this revelation to be received, this authority acknowledged? St Paul's answer, and it is an answer which has nothing in it peculiarly Pauline, is that no man can say "Jesus is Lord", but by the Holy Spirit. In the Old Testament, the Spirit is the power of Jehovah present and working in chosen men. The Spirit is not something different from God, but it is God manifesting himself in a special way—the way of indwelling, or (as we call it) immanence. In the New Testament, the Spirit is this same immanent power of God, present in Jesus the Messiah and imparted by him to his people to possess and unite them with himself. The difference from the Old Testament is simply that now the indwelling power of God is inseparable from the confession of Christ: the Spirit is not the same as the risen and exalted Jesus, but his presence in the whole body of believers replaces the outward presence of Jesus, and supplies all the guidance and strength which outward presence could give. In fact, the belief that what enables us to confess Christ and to follow him in all godliness of living is nothing less than the real presence of God within us—this belief makes the Christian doctrine of Grace inseparable from the doctrine of the Godhead of the Holy Spirit. Christian life is wholly dependent upon the power of the Spirit, because the Spirit is bearer of the Lordship of Jesus, which is the one Lordship of God.

"So the Father is Lord, the Son is Lord, and the Holy Ghost Lord; and yet there are not three Lords but one Lord." In that phrase of the *Quicunque vult*, at least, there is nothing but what can claim "certain warrant" in Holy Scripture. But it falls short of the doctrine of Three Persons in One Substance, distinguished as Persons by their distinct relations to one another. That doctrine, with its technical terms, emerged from the rejection of rival forms of teaching which were professedly designed to maintain the biblical faith in the unity of God. On one side was the Sabellian theory of a Trinity which was not eternal but temporal—no more than the manifestation of the one God through the historic "economy" or dispensation, under the successive forms and by the successive actions of Christ and the Spirit. This was a theory which removed all offence to rational comprehension. But it ran contrary to the fundamental Christian understanding of man's reconciliation to God in Christ. That reconciliation is a reality, not because God has shown us, in Christ's human life of obedient sonship, the pattern of how we are to live as children of the Father in heaven, but because the possibility for us of becoming our Father's sons is given to us by union with Christ; and union with Christ is union with one whose sonship to God is no transient human relationship but an eternal fact of the divine nature. Opposed to Sabellianism was the Arian theory in its various forms, more acceptable to the imperfectly Christianized mind of the Greek because it frankly presented divinity as a matter of degree. Absolute, supreme Godhead belongs only to the changeless, eternal being of the Father: Son and Spirit are subordinate and minor deities, brought into existence to serve the Father's purpose in creation and redemption. In effect, the Arians were abandoning the biblical monotheism which they professed to defend; for the worship which they allowed to Christ was idolatry if Christ was less than very God. But they were abandoning at the same time (as Athanasius so clearly saw) the biblical faith that salvation belongeth unto God. If to be saved is to have eternal life, that is a gift that cannot come to us from one who does not himself possess the eternal life he is to impart.

It was thus a true appreciation of the faith of the New Testament that led the Church to reject both Sabellian and Arian interpretations, however faulty the exegesis of texts by which the rejection was supported. The final decision upon the doctrinal dispute—the dogma of the Trinity—was virtually contained in the application of the single non-biblical word *Homo-ousios*, "of one substance", first at Nicaea in 325 to Christ and afterwards at Constantinople in 381/2 to the whole Trinity. The further elaboration of the doctrine was the working out of the implications of the dogma. Obviously, the emphasis of the dogma is upon the unity of God: what the *Homo-ousios* asserts is not the distinction of the Persons but the one-ness of being. But God reveals his being in his works: the activity of God in creation and redemption, what he *does*, is the expression of what he *is*: the one-ness of his being implies the one-ness of his operation. If then in each Person of the Trinity there is the fullness of God's being, there can be no act of God which is not the act of all three Persons: *Opera Trinitatis ad extra indivisa sunt*. The doctrine of the Trinity cannot *mean*, either that God is Power, Wisdom, and Love (or any other triad of attributes), or that creation, redemption, and sanctification have separate agents in the three Persons of the Godhead. The only difference between the Persons is the difference in the relations in which they stand to one another; and about that we have no light but what is reflected from the Names given to them in Scripture: the Father, from whom are all things, the Son, Word and Image of the Father, through whom are all things, and the Spirit, Gift of both, in whom are all things.

The dogma, as defined, stops there; and no further development of doctrine can *claim* acceptance. Augustine, followed by the Schoolmen, takes the biblical conception of man's making in the image of God to justify his psychological analogy of the human Ego and its three-fold life. Some modern theologians are prepared to take the word Person in a sense in which it was not originally applied, and to defend a view of the Trinity as a divine Society on the ground that personality implies reciprocity, and that the God who is Love is imaged for us in the human family rather than in the human individual. But all such teachings remain speculative unless they can show that no *other* doctrine is compatible with the dogma. The defence of the dogma, as we have seen, can properly rest upon the biblical revelation.

I have tried to suggest, in this example, the sort of connecting lines that *may* be traced between the New Testament as we read it to-day, and the dogmatic orthodoxy of the Ecumenical Councils of the Church; and I believe it would be possible to show similar lines of connection in the case of other doctrines. If our modern understanding of the central message of the New Testament, which we call the Gospel, is reached by methods of interpretation different from those employed in the Church of the Fathers, it is equally true that we find ourselves compelled to interpret the Church's doctrinal formulations in terms which would have been impossible for the Fathers themselves. If we no longer believe that the writers of the New Testament were exempt from the human liability to error, we can hardly be disposed to claim such exemption for the theologians of the fourth century. Yet we may still believe that in the fourth century as in the first, the Holy Spirit was bearing his witness through fallible men to the Christ in whom we have our knowledge of God. The guidance of the Holy Spirit is not indeed to be identified with the *communis sensus fidelium*, to which Christian doctrine has always had to commend itself. That "common sense" is based still, as it always was, in part on familiarity with the text of Scripture, and in part on the practice of common worship and devotion. Doctrine now as always must keep in touch with both if it is to serve not only for the intellectual satisfaction of the learned but for the edification of the Church. For it is through both, through the written word of the Bible and the spoken word of the worshipping community, that the Spirit can speak to every age in its own language of the wonderful works of God.

4

THE MEANING OF
"BIBLICAL THEOLOGY"[1]

GERHARD EBELING

THE PURPOSE of this paper is to set a question-mark against the
concept of "biblical theology"; not to reject it *a priori*, but to
inquire into its meaning, that is, to disclose the problems which
are contained in the concept "biblical theology". The main point of
my observations will therefore lie not so much in answering as in
formulating the question : What is "biblical theology"? For much
is achieved if theologians of widely differing standpoints reach an
understanding of the precise nature of a problem. This is a pre-
requisite for any useful co-operation towards solving it.

"Biblical theology" is in any event no simple idea. It means either
"the theology contained in the Bible", "the theology of the Bible
itself", or "theology in accordance with the Bible, scriptural theology". Both possible meanings are pregnant with a mass of problems.
To comprehend this rightly, we must consider as a basic problem
the relation of these two possible meanings of "biblical theology".
William Wrede was of another opinion. In his book *Ueber Aufgabe
und Methode der sogenannten neutestamentlichen Theologie* (1897),
he makes this distinction of meaning, but only to set it aside as un-
interesting and of no importance. "The name 'Biblical Theology' ",
he says, "originally means not a theology which the Bible has, but
the theology which has a biblical character, and is drawn from the
Bible. For us this is a matter of indifference."[2] I would hold, on the

---

[1] A paper read at the conference of the Society for the Study of Theology
at Oxford, 30 March 1955; reprinted from *J.T.S.*, N.S., Vol. VI, Pt 2, October
1955. [2] Wrede, p. 79.

contrary: for us this is certainly not a matter of indifference. For at this point we touch the real root of the problem, What is biblical theology? In the latter sense "biblical theology" is a normative concept, in the former sense it is an historical concept. In the one "biblical theology" means a theology of the right kind, in the other a theology of a particular historical stamp. Among theologians it is the dogmatic theologian who is concerned with the one, the historical theologian with the other. Even if we take these contrasts as a merely provisional characterization, it is clear that we cannot be content only to distinguish the two meanings of "biblical theology". The burning question is: What is the connection between them and at what points does the one pass over into the other? What is the relation here of dogmatic and historical theology? And what about the relation of the Bible and theology in view of the juxtaposition of a dogmatic and an historical concern with holy Scripture?

If we first consider the phrase "biblical theology" as such, without regard to its origin and the changes in the way it has been understood, we could by starting from naïve presuppositions propose for the sake of argument two opposed ideas. First, this phrase appears to be a tautology. For theology (we presuppose that it is Christian theology) must be in agreement with the Bible if it is to be Christian theology at all. This principle also holds good for Roman Catholic theology. In spite of the fact that tradition ranks as an independent source of revelation beside Scripture, in Roman Catholic thought it is *a priori* impossible that the relation between the two should be a contradiction. Admittedly in this case the designation "biblical theology" would not be a satisfactory definition of the nature of theology, but the accusation of an unscriptural theology contradicting holy Scripture would meet with a decided denial from the Roman Catholic side. The point in dispute within Christian theology is not the fact but the way in which theology is related to the Bible. Only if the latter is more narrowly defined can we advance farther with the phrase "biblical theology". But we could also (for the sake of argument) hold the opposite opinion: the phrase "biblical theology" appears to be a *contradictio in adiecto*. For if the Bible itself is theology in its content, how can its normative, revelatory character be reconciled with the fact that the Bible does not absolve us of the task of studying theology? And if the Bible is not theology at least in its actual content, does not theology necessarily mean a departure from the Bible, a transformation of its content into something which is not strictly in accord with the Bible? If the formula "biblical theology" is to be meaningful, we must explain the presuppositions on which the contradictory character of this tension disappears.

It will, however, be advisable not to go farther with this line of argument, but to seek help in the history of the concept "biblical theology". Certainly, the history of the concept will not simply relieve us from the need for our own reflection. For if it enables us to trace the historical changes through which the idea has hitherto passed, yet it does not provide us with our decision, but only with the material for our decision. But it is a mistake to say that the concepts are a matter of relative indifference, and that we should rather concentrate on the thing itself. The history of the idea is not merely a matter of purely formal questions of nomenclature, but is of high value for understanding the thing itself.

The *terminus a quo* for the occurrence of the concept "biblical theology" is, first, the time at which we first find the idea of "theology" used to designate explanatory teaching of the Christian faith. Surprisingly enough this first occurs in the twelfth century.[3] But I defer for brief discussion later the importance of the history of the concept of "theology" for our problem. A further limitation of the *terminus a quo* for the occurrence of the concept "biblical theology" is provided by the period at which it became possible and necessary to append the epithet "biblical" as a criterion to the concept of "theology", with polemical intention. We might conjecture that this happened in the sixteenth century. The slogan of a "biblical theology" would not be inappropriate for certain biblicist tendencies in Humanism, above all in Erasmus. With much greater probability we might expect it in the reformers to express their biblical principles. Might not Luther's theology—to take him as a brief illustration—be best summed up under the formula "biblical theology"? There is his radical attack upon the authority of tradition and of the Church being set beside, which means that it is set above, that of Scripture; his struggle against the scholastic method in theology and against the influence of Aristotle; the

[3] Here I refer only to the article "Théologie" in *Dictionnaire de Théologie catholique*, xv. 1 (Paris, 1946).

exclusive concentration of his theological work on the exegesis
of holy Scripture; his incomparably profound instinct for the
peculiarities of biblical usage and biblical ways of thinking. In fact
one is bound to say that Reformation theology is the first serious
demand made in the entire history of theology for a theology based
on holy Scripture alone. Only among the followers of the Reformation could the concept "biblical theology" have been coined at all.
Indeed, the process leading to the coining of this idea is obviously
inevitable. And in all that is to be said further on the problem of
"biblical theology" this must be kept in view : we are dealing with
a road which the Reformation made possible, towards which it
pointed, and indeed which it made necessary, even though it was
to become a dangerous threat even for the theology beholden to the
Reformation.

Nevertheless, to the best of my knowledge, the phrase "biblical
theology" is not a creation of the sixteenth century. With reference
to Luther I venture to affirm this with fair certainty and believe that
good reasons can be given for this apart from the mere fact that it
has not been discovered in his writings. Luther was no biblicist. This
is shown by his distinction of Scripture and Christ as well as by the
hermeneutic relevance of his differentiation of law and gospel.
"Scriptura est non contra, sed pro Christo intelligenda, ideo vel ad
eum referenda, vel pro vera scriptura non habenda." "Si adversarii
scripturam urserint contra Christum, urgemus Christum contra
scripturam." "Si utrum sit amittendum, Christus vel Lex, Lex est
amittenda, non Christus."[4] No biblicist speaks like this. What pre-
vented Luther from adopting the only apparently simple formula
of a "biblical theology" was his insight into the hermeneutic
problem.

Admittedly we must judge that Luther's insight into the hermeneutic problem was limited in so far as he had not thoroughly
thought it through from a methodological point of view, and on
that account the methodology of theology remained obscure in
decisive questions of fundamental importance. It was not clear what
the principle of *sola scriptura* would mean for the procedure of
theology as a whole. This obscurity is apparent in the degree to
which Reformation theology, like medieval scholasticism, also

---

[4] D. Martin Luthers Werke, *Kritische Gesamtausgabe* (Weimar, 1883 ff. =
WA), vol. 39, 1; 47, 3 f., 19 f., 23 f. (Disputation theses *de fide* of 11. ix. 1535.)

developed into a scholastic system. What was the relation of this systematic method to the exegetical method? Ultimately it was the same as in medieval scholasticism. There also exegesis of holy Scripture was studied not only within systematic theology, but also separately, yet so that the possibility of a tension between exegesis and systematics was *a priori* excluded. Exegesis was enclosed within the frontiers fixed by systematics, and therefore also theology in the strict sense was the total explication of Christian doctrine, pursuing systematic procedure and normative for exegesis. In this, medieval and old protestant scholasticism are completely similar. Hence also the agreement of both in using Aristotelian philosophy despite Luther's passionate fight against Aristotle's domination of theology. Old protestant orthodoxy could only understand this as an individual eccentricity of Luther's, confined to himself, as also his absolute rejection of the systematic scholastic method in favour of exegesis, though for Luther both belonged inseparably together and were of fundamental importance: "Cum vocabula physica in theologiam translata sunt, facta est inde scholastica quaedam theologia."[5] But just as for Luther himself this primacy of exegesis remained in the last analysis obscure from a methodological point of view (actually there is here an incorporation of the task of systematic theology in exegesis, and thus not a simple antithesis of exegesis and systematics in the modern sense), so also in old protestant orthodoxy the primacy of systematics was in no way connected with an awareness of a departure from the Reformation starting-point. And from an historical point of view we must judge as necessary the intense concern of orthodoxy with the problem of systematic theology on the basis of the Reformation, even though there are strong objections to the orthodox solution of this problem.

The methodological problem contained of necessity in protestantism, as we have seen, but at first only deferred, namely, the implications of the Reformation principle of *sola scriptura* for the procedure of theology as a whole, finally emerged at the moment when the insufficiency and danger of the theological methods of old protestant orthodoxy became apparent. This critical reflection, which started and became articulate within orthodoxy itself and at the same time became the precursor of pietism, established itself in the last analysis with the demand for a "biblical theology", now for

[5] *WA* 39, 1; 229, 22 ff. (Disputation of 1. vi. 1537.)

the first time advanced *expressis verbis*. On this point it is naturally
of extraordinary difficulty to find precise statistics; but subject to
better information I would hold it as a probable conjecture that the
expression "biblical theology" originated about the middle of the
seventeenth century. The oldest instance known to me is a funeral
oration delivered at Tübingen in 1669 for the Württemberg court
preacher Christoph Zeller. According to this report, on the occasion
of a parliament at Regensburg in 1652, Zeller held a conference with
the chief court preacher (*Oberhofprediger*) of Saxony, Jacob Weller,
de Theologia Scholastica which had been expelled by Luther
through the front door but had been reintroduced obviously through
the back door by quarrelsome theologians, and also *de revocanda
Theologia Biblica*. Spener quoted this remark in passing in his *Pia
Desideria* of 1675,[6] and later also took over himself the antithesis of
"biblical theology" and "scholastic theology".[7] It would be of
interest to go more closely into the various trends and traditions
which brought about the origin of pietism in order to trace the
historical roots and perhaps to discover an earlier occurrence of the
concept "biblical theology". But that must be left on one side here.

For understanding the concept "biblical theology" in the period
of its origin the following point is significant: it is the slogan of a
programme of theological reform which directs its criticism neither
at the content of orthodox dogmatics nor at their methodological
form as systematic theology but only at certain accretions, namely
that, as Spener says, "much has been introduced into theology
which is alien, useless, and savours more of the wisdom of the
world",[8] "inquisitive subtleties in matters where we ought not to
enquire beyond the scripture",[9] so that the students become "*studiosi*
of, so to speak, a philosophy *de rebus sacris*, but not *studiosi theologiae*".[10] The dominant theology may "indeed have preserved the
foundation of the faith on scripture, but has built thereon so much
wood, hay, and stubble of human curiosity that one can scarcely
see any more the gold".[11] "The whole of *Theologia*" must therefore

6 Philipp Jacob Spener, *Pia Desideria*, edited by Kurt Aland in *Kleine Texte
für Vorlesungen und Uebungen*, ed. by Hans Lietzmann, no. 170 (Berlin, 1940),
pp. 25 f.

7 e.g. P. J. Spener, *Theologische Bedencken* (Halle, 1715), iv, p. 458.

8 *Pia Desideria*, p. 22, 13 f.

9 p. 22,34 f.   10 p. 71,20 ff.   11 p. 26,36 ff.

"come back again to apostolic simplicity",[12] to the "true simplicity of Christ and his teaching".[13] Thus the catchword "biblical theology" is not advanced to propagate a new theological discipline, nor to shift the centre of gravity from systematics to exegesis (though this was a strong element in pietism). It is rather a demand for the reform of systematic theology itself, and indeed, as it seems, in accordance with its own admitted principles; to some extent it is only a demand for a reform of the style and ethos of theology. It is true that this demand makes its appeal on the ground of a comparison between the Bible, especially the New Testament, and the contemporary form of systematic theology. But the same result arises from the comparison of orthodox with Reformation theology. In both cases the recognized ideal is that of simplicity.[14] Thus the difference in no sense affects the orthodox foundation; the demand for a "biblical theology" in this first stage remains completely on orthodox ground, in so far as it has no doubts about the substantial equation of holy Scripture, Reformation doctrine, and orthodox dogmatic. Orthodox dogmatic is unscriptural only in respect of its scholastic form. But this apparently quite innocuous criticism has much more far-reaching consequences than were immediately perceived. It conceals within itself the seed of a theological revolution, for the varying history of which the slogan "biblical theology" remained a prominent feature.

The momentous importance of this newly coined phrase "biblical theology", which had a strongly reformed ring and against which the dominant orthodox dogmatics could raise no objections, stands in remarkable contrast to the theological naïvety with which the catchword was used. For it was not recognized at all that it was precisely the apparent limitation to a purely formal critique of orthodox scholasticism which had raised the fundamental problem of the methodology of Reformation theology. With appeal to Luther's fight against Aristotle, criticism was levelled at the influence of philosophy upon theology; but they did not consider the problem whether systematic theology is possible without contact with philosophy. For the first time since the Reformation, the Bible on the one hand and the dominant form of theology on the other were regarded as in tension with one another, even though only in a formal respect.

[12] p. 74,5 f.   [13] p. 27,2.   [14] pp. 74,5 f.; 27,2; 22.31.

But they did not reflect at all upon the hermeneutic problem, whether such a tension in one form or another does not always characterize the relation of text and exposition. And they failed to notice that through this elevation of Scripture to the rank of a formal example for theology the criterion of what was in accord with Scripture was silently transposed from the notion of a correct theological understanding to the ideal of theological simplicity. Behind this there stood the opinion in itself orthodox but now used against orthodoxy, that revelation is a sum of revealed doctrines and that the Bible is a theological compendium dictated by the Holy Spirit himself.

The extent to which at the beginning the concept "biblical theology" stood in the twilight of orthodoxy and pietism is shown by the fact that the strongly orthodox Lutheran, Abraham Calov, was able at just the same period to take over this idea and to use it to designate what had hitherto been described as *theologia exegetica*.[15] In this point he fully shared the stronger emphasis of the biblical tendency in theology, as it was expressed in the earliest instance, mentioned above, for the occurrence of the concept "biblical theology". Here, in fact, there are close biographical connections. For Calov was called to Wittenberg through the mediation of the chief court preacher (*Oberhofprediger*) of Dresden, Weller, and later also expressed his warm approval of Spener's *Pia Desideria*. Thus the demand for a "biblical theology" could apparently be included within the orthodox system without reservations; for example, as the use of the analytic method in systematics increased, a need was felt for a separate account of the biblical foundation of dogmatics, and in the so-called *Collegia biblica* the biblical *dicta probantia* for the individual dogmatic *Loci* were collected together. This subsidiary discipline of dogmatics, originating in the second half of the seventeenth century, was given the express title "Biblical Theology" (for the first time in a work of this kind) by Carl Haymann in 1708, though admittedly the growing influence of pietism was at work here. But there is not yet any conscious antithesis to the orthodox treatment of this discipline. Pietism showed itself to be incapable of drawing from the concept "biblical theology" the decisive

[15] Abraham Calov, *Systema theologicum* (1655), i, p. 9. Cp. Ludwig Diestel, *Geschichte des Alten Testaments in der christlichen Kirche* (Jena, 1869), p. 710.

methodological consequences which, as we have seen, were contained in germ within it from the beginning.

These consequences first became evident when the theology of the Enlightenment quite logically took up the catchword of "biblical theology". How easy the transition was is shown by Anton Friedrich Büsching, who lay under the stimulus of pietism but belonged entirely to the so-called Neology, and was a contemporary and associate of the most important German theologian of the eighteenth century, Johann Salomo Semler. Büsching appears only to be resuming the original early pietist demand when he composed a book with the title *Gedanken von der Beschaffenheit und dem Vorzuge der biblisch-dogmatischen Theologie vor der scholastischen* (1758); and he appears to be continuing the late orthodox discipline of a separate account of the scriptural basis of dogmatics in his *Dissertatio exhibens epitomen theologiae e solis literis sacris concinnatae* (1756). Yet at this point the decisive change occurred. From being a merely subsidiary discipline of dogmatics "biblical theology" had achieved a status concurrent with the dominant dogmatics, and although it was itself not something different from dogmatics, yet it was a dogmatic theology which was biblical and not scholastic, a dogmatic which in pursuit of the ideal of the "simple gospel" freed itself from the ballast of dogmatic tradition, which in giving an account of Christian doctrine could even disregard the confessional documents of the Reformation and base its construction only on the purely biblical texts. The conflict in which Büsching thereupon became involved with the Göttingen theological faculty and with the government,[16] proves that the slogan "biblical theology" had now emerged from its original twilight and was to undergo a development which pietism had admittedly inaugurated but of the consequences of which it could have had no notion.

It was now impossible to call a halt. Likewise it was only the logical corollary when under the influence of incipient historical criticism biblical dogmatic, thus given independence over against traditional dogmatic, became aware also of its independence over against dogmatic in regard to its methodology and thereafter remained content neither with the role of a merely subsidiary discipline to dogmatics nor with that of a concurrent variety of dog-

[16] Emanuel Hirsch, *Geschichte der neuern evangelischen Theologie*, iv, (Gütersloh, 1952), pp. 102 f.

matics, but set itself up as a completely independent study, namely as a historical and critical discipline beside dogmatics. It is well known that this was first set forth as a programme by Johann Philipp Gabler in his *Oratio de iusto discrimine theologiae biblicae et dogmaticae regundisque recte utriusque finibus* (1787). But what is now the meaning of "biblical theology" as an historical discipline side by side with dogmatics? A juxtaposition without contact was obviously and self-evidently impossible. For like "biblical theology" as an historical and theological discipline, dogmatics as a systematic and theological discipline must remain tied to the Bible. Accordingly there came into being an extraordinarily difficult coexistence; not only was the relation between the two a matter of continuous controversy, but also, because of this controversy, both the new discipline of "biblical theology" and the traditional discipline of dogmatics were involved in a rapid movement of development and change. Since the idea of "biblical theology" was originally conceived only as a reform of systematic theology, its complete emancipation from dogmatics of necessity had greater and even revolutionary repercussions upon it. Although by this change the theme of "biblical theology" seems to suggest that all our attention should now turn towards the development of this historical discipline and its methodological problems, yet since the Enlightenment the really acute difficulties of theology have lain in the methodological problems of dogmatics.

The relation of "biblical theology" as an historical discipline to dogmatics from now on, despite all variations, remains throughout dominated by the following apparently self-contradictory tendencies. First, as an historical discipline it rejects any directions being laid down for its work which comes from dogmatics. It sees as its vocation that the independence of its historical method, which it proclaims as its principle, should also be realized in detail by emancipation from the traditional dogmatic viewpoint. It has even attempted to justify its existence as an independent theological discipline by discovering more and more new and radical anti-traditional theories. This does not exclude a hesitation between an extreme critical and a cautious conservative position. However, the impulses which really lead to advance in the development of this discipline are beyond question those which sharpen the tension with traditional dogmatics. This is rooted in the law by which "biblical theology" entered the field as a theological discipline. It necessarily adopts a critical attitude to dogmatics. Further, the more "biblical theology" as an historical discipline derives its vitality from its detachment from dogmatics, the less it can be indifferent to the utterances of dogmatics. Even when its lack of interest in systematic theology is most apparent, yet it must at least elevate the claim to be respected by dogmatics. This is true not only in the negative sense that dogmatics should refrain from any interference in the historical study of the Bible, but also in the positive sense that dogmatics, so far as it appeals to the Bible, must bow to the results of historical knowledge of the Bible. What dogmatic theology does with it is its own affair. "Biblical theology" as an historical discipline has for its part no intention of encroaching upon the proper business of dogmatics. Its attitude to dogmatics remains that of a detached spectator, often not without compassionate amusement at the embarrassments in which dogmatic theology finds itself. It is to be left with the doubtful advantage of providing normative theological statements for the contemporary situation, while the student of historical theology thinks he can confine himself to establishing merely historical facts. Yet there is no escape from the fact that "biblical theology" as an historical discipline exercises a normative function over against dogmatics in all matters concerning the relation to the Bible. Dogmatics must render account of its use of Scripture before the judgement seat of historical study of the Bible. Lastly, we must not lose sight of the fact that although "biblical theology" as an historical discipline adopts this detached attitude to traditional dogmatics, while at the same time claiming a critical and normative function, it remains itself dogmatically interested to a high degree, even (and indeed most decisively) where this fact is not granted. Since its origin the appeal of the name of this discipline has been that it is a guide to the real, original, and pure source of theological knowledge. This imparted to it a claim which, especially in the field of Reformation theology, could hardly be challenged. But through its necessarily critical attitude towards traditional dogmatics "biblical theology" recognized above all the untenability of the very presupposition from which it had itself started, namely the orthodox doctrine of verbal inspiration. "Biblical theology" as an historical discipline, in its critical debate with dogmatics, had to begin at once precisely at the point at which as a separate discipline it was itself in dogmatic fetters. Its critical inclination over against dogmatics thus touched "biblical theology" at its foundation. The result was a fresh awareness of its foundation, that is, of the basis and nature of the authority of holy Scripture. Because "biblical theology" had become an historical discipline, this fresh consideration of its foundation did not proceed in the traditional dogmatic manner, but partly by general consideration of the scientific method in history and the nature of historical knowledge, partly by fuller study of the biblical text itself. But this did not mean that in this work definite dogmatic positions were not adopted. For anyone who as an historian concerns himself with "biblical theology" does this with knowledge of the relevance of holy Scripture for Christian faith and because of this relevance. Therefore it is not merely a matter of fact, it is so because it cannot be otherwise, that the general methodological reflection upon the task and nature of "biblical theology" as an historical discipline implies a particular understanding of the Christian faith and the importance of the Bible for it, and that the actual results of research are determined by the question to which they are the answer; and this question is dependent upon a certain insight into the subject-matter of the Bible. That is, "biblical theology" as an historical discipline is like any historical work not independent of the stand-point of the author, and therefore also not of the conception which the author has of the Christian faith—a conception which in its general structure is of a dogmatic kind even when in opposition to traditional dogmatic theology it asserts itself to be undogmatic. The history of "biblical theology" provides evidence to show that it reflects the change of the historical, and therefore also the theo-logical, standpoint of the author. In the relations between historical research and theological standpoint there is further opportunity for possibilities of variation in matters of detail, within the entire framework of ideas that has been outlined. Two extremes may be mentioned: in the age of rationalism the outcome of "biblical theology", with the aid of the distinction drawn between the time-conditioned and the timelessly valid, led directly to the character-istic features of a rationalist dogmatic theology. By this method the historical distance from the Bible was eliminated. In the com-parative study of religions (*religionsgeschichtliche Schule*), on the other hand, it is primarily the historical distance which is thrown into relief. As asserting an immediate claim there only remains a vague religious impulse. In both cases, however, there remains in "biblical theology". a dogmatic element inseparably bound up with the historical; in fact because of the conscious exclusion of dogmatic tradition there is always such a dogmatic element, which adopts a more or less critical attitude to this dogmatic tradition.

It is not possible here to trace the history of "biblical theology" as an historical discipline. I confine myself to the question : What contribution is made by the history of the discipline to the explanation of its name? To this the answer is that this history has brought to light for the first time the problem contained in the concept "biblical theology", and that in the following respect. The theological unity of the Bible has become a problem. It soon became evident that it was necessary to divide a discipline of "biblical theology" into two, a theology of the Old Testament and a theology of the New Testament. This has not merely happened in the course of a progressive specialization of historical methods of study, and the division of the field which this has entailed. What theologian of to-day is able to be equally expert in both Old and New Testament studies? The real reason for the division into two disciplines is rather that through the historical criticism of the Bible the theological unity of the Old and New Testaments has become problematic. From an historical point of view it is impossible to regard the statements of the Old and New Testaments as being on one level without any distinction and by combining them together to produce a single theology of the Bible. It is true that at first the designation "biblical theology" forms the common title for accounts of Old and New Testament theology following one after the other in one and the same book. But as this separation also came to achieve outward recognition, the designation "biblical theology" stayed on as a reminiscence of a lost unity in the description of the two disciplines, in that people did not speak simply of an Old Testament or of a New Testament theology, but of a "Biblical Theology of the Old Testament" and a "Biblical Theology of the New Testament". But this manner of speaking did not become established. The title as a designation of a theological discipline has to-day ceased to exist in practice.

The inner unity of the Old and New Testaments has also become a problem. Historical criticism, logically applied to the biblical

writings, increasingly revealed the differences within the two
Testaments and primarily concentrated attention on these. Thus
Old and New Testament theology became an account of various
kinds of theology ordered in historical succession. The description
was diluted to a formal collective idea for ordering under one head
the doctrinal ideas of different biblical writers, without any
narrower definition of the theological unity of the whole being
possible. Even when exaggeration of the difference between the
doctrinal ideas was shown by historical criticism to result from
reading too much into the text which provided too narrow a basis
for it, and the main complexes received primary attention, the unity
of the whole was only treated from the point of view of development. Old and New Testament theology became in practice a history
of Old and New Testament theology. Even when beside or even in
place of the genetic treatment there is a purely systematic classifica-
tion covering the whole (as, for example, in Eichrodt's and Köhler's
theology of the Old Testament, and in Stauffer's *New Testament
Theology*), even so the historical differences must be recognized if
such an account is not to be open to the charge of reducing to a
single level the historical form of the biblical witness. Even where
the inner unity of the Old and New Testaments is expounded, it is
in any event extremely difficult to understand this unity as a
unitary theology, if theology (as distinct from doctrine or credal
confession) has at times a particular individual character and so,
for example, the Pauline and Johannine witness cannot be regarded
as an identical theology.

The limitation to the canon of Scripture has also become
problematic, in the first place because Old and New Testament
studies cannot avoid considering the religious background and must
at least allow the consequence of the comparison to have its effect
upon an Old or New Testament theology; but further, and this is
the decisive point, because for an account of the historical development a limitation to the selection given in the canon is not justified.
If a picture of the total process is really to emerge, an Old Testament
theology can hardly refuse to extend its range beyond the canonical
Scriptures into pre-Christian Judaism. And certainly a New Testament theology cannot overlook the extra-canonical literature of
early Christianity of the same period as the books of the canon. This
breaks the normative viewpoint contained in the idea of the canon;

but, quite apart from that, this has already been abandoned by the application of the methods of historical criticism to the canon itself. For the historical point of view excludes any idea of a canon which implies the hermeneutic rule that the canon is without distinction and in all its parts of the same authority and that discrepancies and contradictions therein are *a priori* excluded.

A further problem is the use of the concept "theology" to apply to the actual content of the Bible. This use of the concept is the common inheritance of medieval and protestant scholasticism according to which revelation consists in the communication of revealed truths; the word of God is identical with theological propositions; theology and revelation or theology and the knowledge of God (or faith) are thus not distinguished from one another in principle and in structure. But this concept of theology has become problematic through the historical discipline of so-called "biblical theology" itself. We may regard it as unfortunate when this has given place to the general notion of religion, and when the concept of an Israelite-Jewish or primitive Christian *Religionsgeschichte* threatens to displace the idea of Old or New Testament theology. But we must in any event recognize the criticism that it expresses, that that whereof the Bible witnesses and which is its object is not theology but something that happens to man between God and the world. Even if we maintain the interpretation of this happening as revelation and faith, we must not abandon the distinction that revelation as such is not theology and faith as such is not belief in theological propositions. The highly questionable orthodox concept of a *theologia revelata* does not hold for the actual content of the Bible. Of course this is not to deny that the Bible contains theology. But the question that arises here is what is to be claimed as theology in the Bible, and that means, what is our idea of theology as we approach the Bible. The fact that the Bible itself does not use the word "theology" is obviously not in itself a reason for not applying it to the Bible. But it is a doubtful proceeding to use the concept theology in such a wide sense that any talk of God and any religious statement whatever may be designated as theology. This extension of the term theology to cover any conglomeration of religious ideas has become usual in modern study of religion, and significantly it has its reverse side in that such a study of religion does not in fact regard itself as theology.

I am of the opinion, which of course I cannot defend in detail here, that from the history of the word "theology" criteria can be derived for its accurate use. It can be shown that theology emerges from the meeting of the witness of the biblical revelation with Greek thought, and that these two elements are constitutive for the nature of theology. From this standpoint it would in fact be meaningful to speak of theology even in the New Testament, above all in Paul and the author of the Fourth Gospel. On the other hand, it would be questionable to describe the preaching of the individual prophets of the Old Testament as theology, though that is certainly capable of theological explication. From this the conclusion follows that although the Bible for the most part does not contain theology in the strict sense, yet it requires a theological explication. From this point of view it could also be meaningful to speak of a theology of the Old or New Testament, so long as the word "theology" did not, or at least did not primarily, describe the content of the Old or New Testament, but rather the scientific explication of what they contain. This alone would also justify the singular "theology". A New Testament theology would be so entitled as a contemporary theological explanation of that which in the New Testament itself points towards such an explanation, or of that which in the New Testament has already the beginnings of a theological explanation, but which nevertheless needs a contemporary interpretation if it is not merely to be repeated but is to achieve a scientific statement. This also explains why the scientific discipline which we call Old and New Testament theology must be studied over and over again. Like all historical study, it is not a photographic reproduction of the past, but an understanding of the past exhibited in a contemporary interpretation. Therefore *the* Old or *the* New Testament theology will never be written. It cannot be written, because in principle the discipline of Old or New Testament theology cannot be finally settled, but constitutes a continually advancing undertaking.

Let us consider our argument. Our question was, what has the history of "biblical theology" as an historical discipline to contribute towards an explanation of the name? Our answer was, that the history has for the first time brought to light the problem contained in the concept "biblical theology". I illustrated this in the problems of the theological unity of the Bible, of the inner unity of the Old and New Testaments, of the limitation to the canon of

Scripture, and of the application of the concept "theology" to the actual content of the Bible. It might appear that the result is the same as that reached by William Wrede, that is, the argument that the history of the concept "biblical theology" is in that respect a *reductio ad absurdum* of the idea. It is true that the understanding of the concept "biblical theology" held at the period of its origin in its original context on the frontier of orthodoxy and pietism underwent refutation and dissolution in the course of its history. There is an inexorable logic in this development. It cannot be remedied by an attempt to drive it back to its starting-point. But this development, as has become clear in the discussion of the problem of the concept "theology" and its application to the actual content of the Bible, contains a pointer which Wrede did not consider and which offers the possibility of seeing the problem in a new light. It would be entirely wrong to interpret the development as mistaken and as having a purely destructive result. It has rather an uncommonly positive importance in that by setting aside all short cuts towards a solution it has led us to the real issue of the hermeneutic problem. Thus it has necessitated thoroughgoing and precise definition of the problem of theological method posed by the Reformation. I venture to affirm that thanks to the evolution of the historical method which has dominated the history of theology since the Enlightenment we are in a better position to achieve a correct understanding of the task of Reformation theology than could be found in old protestant orthodoxy. For we can see more sharply the task for theology which arises from holy Scripture. I do not mean that we have ready to hand solutions with which we can be satisfied, but that we can see problems before us and can take heart that we can see what they are.

The implication of this for the theme of this paper in a narrower sense can only be outlined; for there at once arises a mountain of labour, which has not yet been conquered.

The task of a theology of the Old or New Testaments is, in view of what has been said concerning the concept of theology, to be defined as follows: The theologian who dedicates himself specially to research in the Old or New Testaments has to give an inclusive account of his understanding of the Old or New Testaments, that is, above all of the theological problems which arise from the fact that

6

the variety of the biblical witness is considered in relation to its inner unity.

From this definition the question would arise whether a discipline of "biblical theology" is not in fact possible and indeed necessary. Its task would accordingly be defined thus: In "biblical theology" the theologian who devotes himself specially to studying the connection of the Old and New Testaments must give account of his understanding of the Bible as a whole, that is, above all of the theological problems that arise from the variety of the biblical witness considered in relation to its inner unity.

In the contemporary situation of theological study such a "biblical theology" demands intensive co-operation from Old and New Testament scholars. It is not to be expected that it will develop into a separate discipline. It will rather remain a matter of scientific conversation between the two disciplines and will be advanced sometimes more strongly by the one, sometimes by the other. But just as now theology both of the Old and of the New Testaments, in consequence of being involved in the hermeneutic problem, must have close contact with systematic theology since on account of the hermeneutic problem the exegete must participate in the work of systematic theology, so also the appointed task of a "biblical theology" is in increasing measure a contribution to systematic theology, since in this task the hermeneutic problem is extraordinarily complicated. The task of "biblical theology" would then be the compelling impulse towards a close co-operation of the various theological disciplines, from which the church historian cannot be omitted. But, be it noted, this "biblical theology" would not be an independent substitute for dogmatics and would hardly correspond to the pietist ideal of a simple theology, but would be a task for historical theology of uncommon complexity. But it would be able to draw upon the assistance of dogmatics to get a stronger grasp of the question of what is a scriptural dogmatic theology.

Thus the concept "biblical theology", in consequence of the false understanding of which, contrary to the original intention, theology has split up into different disciplines, points when rightly understood towards the restoration of the unity of theology; of course, this is not a unity achieved by abolishing the different disciplines, but a unity consisting in the right theological use of the various disciplines, each one of which has its own task and each of which is "theology" in the manner of its participation in the scientific expression of the word of God. This understanding of the unity of theology in which the historian and the systematic theologian keep an open conversation between them, since the historian must also be a systematic theologian if he is to be an historian, and the systematic theologian must also be an historian if he is to be a systematic theologian, seems to me to be in line with the Reformation understanding of theology. For theology in this sense is never something achieved, is never at its goal. The goal is only achieved by faith or rather by the word of God in that it awakens faith.

5

BIBLE AND TRADITION [1]

C. F. EVANS

IT IS not an infrequent experience in our lives that some activity
from which we had hoped a great deal has disappointed the particular hopes which we had entertained of it, while at the same time
it has brought us something else which we had not been led to
expect, and which turns out to be of far greater value to us than
would have been the fulfilment of our original hope. Something of
this kind has, perhaps, been happening in that branch of theological
study under which the Church has had to learn to live in the last
century or so, and which is more clearly connected with the
work of a university in modern times—the historical criticism and
analysis of the Scriptures and of the Fathers.

The original hopes for historical criticism were lively and definite.
It was hoped, at least in those quarters where it was most vigorously
pursued, that it would break the stalemate which had developed in
Christendom since the Reformation by providing a version of Christianity which should be solidly, because scientifically, based. The
stalemate had been brought about by the Protestant revolt against
Catholic orthodoxy. It had been assumed before the Reformation
that New Testament religion and Catholic orthodoxy were synony-
mous. In fact, while Catholic orthodoxy rested to some extent on
the basis of the New Testament, it had come as a developing system
to interpret the New Testament in ways other than the New Testament itself really allowed. This harmonious development was broken
by the Reformation, and its breaking was defended by the reformers
by recourse to the Bible, and by the claim that, judged by the New

[1] Reprinted from *Theology*, Vol. LX, No. 450 (Jan. 1957), pp. 437-44.

Testament, Catholic orthodoxy was found gravely wanting. The
claim was made that Protestants were true to biblical religion,
Catholicism was not. But Protestants were not content with that;
for they went on to erect doctrinal systems no less than Catholic
orthodoxy. There are not wanting signs that this might not have
been the outcome of the Reformation. There are insights, for
example, in Luther which point in another direction. His rejection
of the allegorical interpretation of the Bible, the criterion which he
applied that "what urges Christ is Scripture though written by
Judas" and "what does not urge Christ is not Scripture though
written by an apostle", by which criterion he judged the Epistle of
James a "right strawy epistle", his view of the Old Testament as
containing in prophecy that which pointed to Christ and in law that
which was intended to convince men of sin; these insights, if
followed up, might have led to a less systematic and more discrim-
inating use of the Bible. But they were not followed up. They were
lost to sight in the busy construction of doctrinal systems, for each
of which it was now claimed that it was *the* biblical system of
theology. In constructing these systems far more was taken over
from Catholic orthodoxy by the reformers than they realized
at the time, and in order to make out of it a system of theology the
Bible had to be interpreted throughout by selecting from it a single
canon of interpretation, in the case of Lutheranism justification by
faith alone, in the case of Calvinism the predestination of the elect,
and again, as in Catholic orthodoxy, some parts were distorted
in the process of making a system out of the whole. Thus
Chillingworth's dictum "the Bible and the Bible only is the religion
of all Protestants" has never been strictly true.

Now these claims of several bodies to possess in their systems the
true biblical theology gave rise to the historical method. This
method asked the question, "What does the Bible mean when considered in its own right, and without reference to any doctrinal
system?" It was the confident hope that it could answer this question and provide a Christianity solidly because scientifically based,
and so break the stalemate of Christendom, which gave such zest
to historical criticism, and led to the constant sharpening of its tools.
This hope has not been fulfilled, and is not likely to be fulfilled.
There has, indeed been much talk of late of an entity called "biblical
theology", but this will probably turn out to be no more than a

temporary excitement over the fact that, after a long period of analysis and breaking up, in which the Bible seemed to have been reduced to a heap of bits, some of the bits have shown a tendency to come together again at another, and perhaps deeper, level. There is, it would seem, not one theology of the Bible, but several theologies in it, and it would also seem that in serving up the results of biblical criticism in the form of biblical theology some canon of interpretation is still at work, and that a canon which is not itself the immediate and automatic product of this criticism. But while this particular hope has been disappointed, may not the historical method have perhaps been producing something else which was not being looked for from the outset, and which may be of greater value in the history of Christendom? For what the critical method may have done is so to have opened up the Bible as to show that it does not contain a system of theology, and is a singularly unpromising foundation for theology considered as a closed system. And it may have done this in two ways.

First, it has recovered from the periphery of Christian thinking and placed at its centre the eschatology of the New Testament. The expectation of an end, the looking forward to a consummation, cannot now be regarded as one department of Christian doctrine, summarized as death, judgement, heaven, and hell, to which we may pay attention in addition to other departments. It is shown rather to be the presupposition of all else; it governs all that is said and done in the New Testament, just as the plus or minus sign which stands outside a bracket determines the value of everything within the bracket. It is the critical analysis of the New Testament that most clearly shows this to be so, and that allows it to have its full force. And Christ himself, who is the centre of the Bible, does not stand outside it; he is himself involved in a passionate eschatology. He labours to establish the kingdom or rule of God among men, proclaims that with him and his ministry among men it has broken in, and yet no less asserts that just because this is so, precisely because it is the rule of God amongst *men*, it must await a consummation and finality, of which he can assure men, but which he cannot produce or guarantee, if to guarantee means to provide it for himself or to know its precise hour and manner. Indeed he is himself the king in the divine kingdom precisely because he, as man, is subject to its rule, and for that reason cannot secure his own consummation, but must await it from God. The last word remains with God. It might perhaps be observed, as an outward and visible sign of this, that no book in the New Testament appears to know how to end. St Mark's Gospel, how does it end? As we have it, with the words "for they were afraid". St Matthew ends by throwing an umbrella over the rest of time: "Go ye into all the world . . . and I am with you unto the end of the ages." Luke-Acts, the most literary work in the New Testament, has an ending which continues to shock the critics, not closing with a flourish and a fine description of the martyrdom of St Paul, but petering out with the rather banal statement that "he remained in his own hired dwelling preaching and teaching with all boldness and without hindrance". St John's Gospel ends with the remark of the author that he supposes that if all the things that Jesus did were to be written down the world would not be able to contain the books which could be written; the Epistles with a blessing tacked on to the last thing the apostle happens to have been talking about, or with "Little children, keep yourselves from idols". And the New Testament itself, how does it end?—with words stretching out to the indefinite future: "Amen: come, Lord Jesus."

In the introduction to his edition of Tolstoy's *War and Peace* Mr Aylmer Maude remarks that *War and Peace* stands at a crucial point where the modern novel begins, and he explains what he means as follows: "Tolstoy created something which may be said to be no longer a novel—it is the open form of the novel as opposed to the closed form. Flaubert in *Madame Bovary* was bringing the closed form to perfection. It has a beginning, a middle and an end, a single jet ending in a definite solution of the conflicts inside the novel. Tolstoy in *War and Peace* transcends the limits of the novel, and does what had previously been done by the epic. It has to be classed with the *Iliad*, in the sense that when the novel is finished nothing is finished—the main stream of life flows on, and with the appearance of Prince Andrew's son the novel ends with the beginning of a new life. All the time there are openings out into the world beyond." The Bible also would seem to have something of this nature, not as the product of literary craft, but by its concentration upon the finality of God.

The more this is allowed to appear, the more the embattled positions of Catholicism and Protestantism which have developed since the Reformation would seem to have been by-passed. For those positions have always tended in the direction of an infallibility, whether of the Church or of the Book. This is not surprising. The longing of the religious man is always for finality. Of course. Do we not come to our rest at length with God, and is not all our language about God in intention final language? But it is the particular temptation of the religious man to snatch at finality when it cannot be had and in the form in which he ought not to have it. The finality of the Christian religion is finality of a highly paradoxical kind. It is not the finality of a sign from heaven, a portent which underwrites and guarantees, or the finality of the wisdom of the Greeks, of a system with all the answers. It is a finality of real incarnation, of real submission to God in the conditions of this world. It is therefore a finality in which nothing is finished. Would there not be, then, something gravely inconsistent if such a Christ on earth were replaced by, or represented by, an organ of Christ, be it Church or Book, which had a finality other than the finality of him whose organ it was? We used to be told: "Beware of any sentence which begins with the words 'if only' because it is a liberal sentence." But we must also beware of any sentence which begins with the words "Surely God would have . . ." for it is a religious *a priori* sentence. "Surely God would have seen to it that the Bible would have been preserved from error." "Surely God would have seen to it that there would be an instrument on earth which would teach without error." This is how the sentences run which are spoken from the embattled positions. But for all their impressiveness must they not be judged irreligious and heretical sentences? For can it not be said that our Lord was crucified by just such a religious *a priori*? Surely God will see to it that when his kingdom is manifested on earth it will carry all before it. Of course—how else? Is it not the kingdom of God that we are talking about, and is not God God? But paradoxically it does not do so, and is not the less the kingdom of God because manifested in apparent lack of power, not as harvest but as seed awaiting harvest, not as lamp already on the lamp stand for all to see but as lamp looking as if it were under a bed, yet destined to be taken out from under the bed. Nothing is finished short of its final consummation at the hands of God. The New Testament is therefore a very un-promising foundation for a system, and it is a religious question of deep moment whether it is God's will that we should live under a system, however valuable such may be to help us on our way.

But if not under a system, under what authority are we to live, and how is the authority or God to be mediated to us? For the Catholic and Protestant systems have not been good for nothing. The conflict between them has been so bitter because it has been a conflict about the authority under which we live, and that is a very intimate matter. On the one hand, the authority of the Book as the unique record and witness of the once for all event in which God is supremely revealed; on the other hand, the ongoing life of the Church in which the continuing and living Lord explicates his revelation and brings it continually to life. In other words, the question of Bible and Tradition. Perhaps here also the critical move-ment in biblical studies may have something to contribute, not by way of agreed solutions or findings, but rather by way of an alteration of perspective, a change in the terms of the conflict. For this question the biblical student finds forced upon him by his studies.

The judgement of the Council of Trent on the matter runs as follows: "The sacred and holy oecumenical and general synod . . . keeping this always in view that the purity of the Gospel be pre-served in the Church, which Gospel promised before through the prophets in the holy scriptures our Lord Jesus Christ first promul-gated with his own mouth, and then commanded to be preached by his apostles to every creature, as the fountain of all saving truth and moral discipline; and seeing clearly that this truth and discipline are contained in the written books and the unwritten traditions which, received by the apostles from the mouth of Christ himself, or from the apostles themselves, the Holy Spirit dictating, have come down to us, transmitted as it were from hand to hand, the synod receives and venerates them with an equal affection of piety and reverence, all the books both of the Old and New Testaments, as also the said traditions, as well those pertaining to faith as to morals, as having been dictated either by Christ's own word of mouth or by the Holy Ghost, and preserved in the Catholic Church by a continuous succession." The Bible, that is, and of equal authority, supplying its lacunae, the traditions.

There are several things which could be said about this; for example, that in the earliest ages the claim to possess special traditions not generally available was a mark of Gnostics, and was vigorously opposed by the Church. But perhaps the most curious thing about it is that it is surprisingly difficult to discover what precisely these traditions are. Inasmuch as they constitute on the Catholic side the nearest thing to Luther's *articulus aut stantis aut cadentis ecclesiae*, one would have expected to have available a convenient list of these traditions, for want of which so many are perishing. Yet the theologians are remarkably fugitive, even coy, about the matter, and when we come across one of such traditions — e.g. that only by tradition do we know that the Christian day of worship is Sunday — we do not need to assume as its basis an actual word of the Lord taken from that most convenient dumping ground for all desirable doctrines, the great forty days after Easter, of which St Luke tantalizingly tells us that the Lord spoke many things about the kingdom of God without saying what any of them were. A satisfactory alternative explanation suggests itself, that it arose naturally out of the supreme importance attached by the first Christians to the Lord's resurrection. Indeed, the practical uselessness of the decree of Trent is indicated by the more recent dogmas pronounced by the Church of Rome, in which the attempt to find their basis in such unwritten traditions handed down in unbroken succession is frankly abandoned, and the place of traditions is taken by tradition, understood now as that which is believed by the present consensus of the faithful. It is difficult to exaggerate the horror of the Protestant at the possibilities of corruption inherent in this vicious circle, whereby the Scriptures are deprived of their power to purify the Church because they are made always to echo the voice of the Church. And he will continue to protest, and to protest with sorrow, when, as it seems to him, he sees the largest and most august body in Christendom thus cutting the knot with history and with the Scriptures, and on the way to becoming what Abbé Loisy was excommunicated for saying it was, the heir to all the mystery religions in the world, the greatest mystery religion of all time, which lives not by any faithfulness to a Jesus of history but by the worship of the Son of God and by sacraments which produce saints.

On the other side, opposing Trent, the Bible and the Bible only.
All else is secondary and to taste. The Holy Scriptures contain all
things necessary for salvation. Yet has it ever worked quite like
that? A child is born and is brought to regeneration and to membership of Christ's Church by infant baptism, concerning which the
Scriptures say nothing, and in protest against which one body of
Christians stands apart. It is nurtured by prayers, most of which
come to him from the spiritual experience of his forefathers. He is
brought to confirmation at the hands of a bishop, of both of which
the Scriptures say nothing certain, and both of which are repudiated
by many. Through confirmation he is to come to the regular
participation in the sacrament of Christ's Body and Blood, of which
indeed the Scriptures say important things, but that it is to be
the weekly, even daily, pleading of Christ's sacrificial death and
the central point of the Church's worship is the judgement of the
corporate mind of the Church and not the express statement of the
Scriptures. In all these things, no doubt, the Bible stands in the background guarding the truth, but our initiation into these things as
living things is through the living Church, and it is difficult to
exaggerate the horror of the Catholic at the replacement of the
beloved communion of saints, across the world and down the ages,
living and departed, by what seems to him a desert stretching
between the death of the last apostle to write in the Scriptures
and the second coming of the Lord, and ourselves left to find our
way in the desert only by the reading and preaching of the word.
"If democracy", wrote Chesterton, "means that I give a man a vote
despite the fact that he is my chauffeur, tradition means that I give
a man a vote despite the fact that he is my great-great grandfather."
And when my great-great-grandfather means the beloved community
of Christ's brethren that is something very precious.

Clearly both sides in this controversy have been contending for
what is of great importance, and what is characteristic of both
sides is that they have thought of themselves as operating with fixed,
circumscribed, and rigid entities. On the one hand, the Bible, firmly
sealed at both ends, a book of uniform divinity throughout, the end
implicit, or even explicit, in the beginning; on the other hand,
tradition, an ascertainable number of teachings and practices,
marching parallel with Scripture and supplying its lacunae. It
is the precision of this picture which historical criticism makes

it difficult to sustain. For the Bible is now as it were open at both ends. Emerging from a mist of legend at one end, departing in a haze of apostolic pseudonymity at the other, the canon of Scripture can hardly be taken by us with that deadly seriousness with which our forefathers have taken it. Further, between the beginning and the end the analysis of the Scriptures has made us aware, at every turn, of the Church. I do not simply mean that it has made us aware of the existence of the Church as part of the Gospel and not a convenience added to it— although that also is the case—but something deeper than that. It has made us aware of the continuing life of the Church in the first century as the very matrix out of which it has pleased God to give us his word. We are made aware that the Scriptures contain patterns of preaching, forms of catechetical instruction, embryo creeds, which have already taken shape and been formulated before the writers in whose writings they now appear put pen to paper. There is evidence that the liturgical worship of the Church has already had something to do with moulding what we are reading. We are made aware that we cannot have a parable simply as the Lord may have told it, but only through the medium of Christians who, because it was their present and living Lord who had spoken it, have applied it to their own circumstances, in the firm conviction that the same Lord was speaking to those circumstances. We are made aware, as in the Fourth Gospel, that we can only have what the Lord said and did as seen in the light of, and in a measure identified with, that Christian life and experience which emerged out of what he said and did, so that the two can no longer be disentangled. The more the New Testament is taken to bits the more it leads us back to a preaching, teaching, worshipping, and living Church as the background of all its parts and as the setting in which alone they come alive. We are brought into touch with a transcript of a tradition which is constantly in movement. The word preached evokes response, the response is itself assimilated into the preaching or teaching, and at the next stage or level the preaching or teaching cannot be had apart from the response. It begins to look as if the New Testament is like an iceberg, four-fifths submerged and one-fifth visible. We are aware of the existence of the four-fifths submerged, although we do not know precisely what it is; but the knowledge that it is there as the basis of the one-fifth which is visible is important, if the manner in which the Scriptures were created and given to us is to have any bearing on the manner in which they are to be received and used. For it is not now the Bible and Tradition alongside each other, or over against each other, but tradition within the Bible, the Bible itself largely tradition.

This is of course to give to tradition a less precise meaning than it has generally held, and we shall need the researches of our theologians to tell us whether and how it is to be filled out, but this would seem to be the form of the question with which we shall have to live for some time to come, as it is posed to us by biblical studies. And perhaps not by biblical studies only. Writing as a scholar in patristics, in which field I have no sort of competence to judge, Père Bouyer, of the Roman obedience, makes the following statements:[2] To attempt to arrive at a one-sided answer to the question of Scripture and Tradition is doomed to failure, since the Fathers can quite cheerfully say at one moment that the whole of the faith is contained in the Scriptures, and at another with equal confidence that Scripture is of no avail without tradition as its complement or supplement, and they are able to speak like this because they do not, as we have tended to do, whether Catholic or Protestant, think of the faith as a list of propositions of divinity, but as a unity, a single living object under multiple forms. Moreover, they do not mean by Scripture primarily an authority under which we live, but a whole world in which we live, and everything in the world to be read through it, and the whole world to be found in it. This wholeness, without which neither the spirit nor the letter of Scripture can be grasped, is proliferated in the living Gospel of the Church, which, though always consonant with Scripture, is not dependent upon it, and its purpose is to prevent us from maiming the data of Scripture through a minimizing or distorted interpretation. And he concludes with two points: (i) the Christian faith objectively speaking is a deposit once and for all committed in its fullness to the Church, and that fullness is for ever supremely attainable in Scripture; (ii) this same object is not to be grasped anywhere else than in the Church itself, in which channel it is transmitted in conformity with the living manner in which the life of the Church itself is disseminated.

2 *The Eastern Churches Quarterly*, Vol. VII, Supplementary Issue.

Whether this is a view which will stand up to the scrutiny of his fellow scholars in a subject notoriously complex I do not know. It is a view which in its own way escapes in considerable measure from the embattled positions which have kept the stalemate of the last four hundred years in being; it is also a view which, approaching from the Fathers, approximates to the picture of the Bible which would seem to be emerging from modern study. On this view our problem will not be only, or perhaps primarily, the problem of the unity of a Bible which has been pulled to bits, but of a living whole of tradition which, in a divided Christendom, has become a fragmented whole. But since the living whole of tradition, including that living whole which is the Bible, has become what it is by a process of growth—to use Père Bouyer's words, "by the vital manner in which the life of the church is disseminated in time and space"—are we forbidden to hope that it may come together again into unity by growth; not the inevitable growth of the biological kind, growth presumably under the Holy Spirit, but nevertheless growth?

6

WHEREIN LIES THE AUTHORITY
OF THE BIBLE ? [1]

D. E. NINEHAM

I HAVE sometimes offered my students an illustration of this
matter along some such lines as these. Suppose that a friend of
mine were entering on some vital business dealings with a man who
was personally unknown to him. He would obviously want to
know all he could about this man — and he might appeal to me for
help. "Do *you* know so-and-so?" he might ask, "Can *you* tell me at
all what sort of person it is that I shall be dealing with?" I might
have to say that I did not know this person in the sense of ever
having been introduced to him or admitted to his family circle,
or even of knowing his personal habits and peculiarities. I might
even have to say that I had never seen the man and did not know
what he looked like. "And yet," I might say to my friend, "I think
I can help you, for I know certain things that this person has done

---

[1] Professor Nineham writes: "In 1958 I was invited to deliver one of the
Advent Lectures at Sion College. The course had clearly been planned with
the recent Lambeth Conference in mind, and the subject allotted was the
authority of the Bible. Realizing that in the course of a fifty-minute lecture I
could not deal comprehensively with so vast a subject, I decided to limit
myself to a critique of some current views on the subject which, though
widespread and hallowed by tradition, seemed unacceptable in the twentieth
century, and to an attempt to show that in reality the question, "Wherein
lies the authority of the Bible?" admits of no single easily formulated answer.
I was aware that this gave the lecture a predominantly negative tone and for
that reason when I delivered the lecture on Monday, 1 December, I devoted a
few moments at the end to a brief sketch of what seemed the most hopeful
positive approach to the matter. This aspect could not, however, be satis-
factorily treated in so brief a compass, and in this printed version my closing
remarks are omitted

"In connection with several points, particularly on pp. 84 and 91, I should
like to express my indebtedness to some unpublished work by the Reverend
Graham Neville, on which I have been allowed to draw".

© D. E. Nineham, 1960.

which will give you quite a good line upon him." For example,
I might be able to tell my friend how this man had begun with a
very small retail business and had gradually expanded it till he was
one of the most successful manufacturers and richest millionaires
in the country; that would at least show that he was no fool where
business was concerned. But I might also know of an occasion when
this same man had provided expensive medical treatment for one of
his employees at his own cost, or of another occasion when he had
provided a much needed holiday for the family of an old associate.
Or again I might be able to tell how he had once financed out of his
own pocket a whole programme of research upon some particularly
stubborn disease, and then built a special hospital in which the
fruits of this research might be made available in the form of
medical treatment. All this would reveal him, not only as a man of
vast resources, but as a man of great generosity and goodwill, deeply
concerned about the needs and sufferings of his fellows.

In this way I might be able to help my friend; and it is important
to see why. Not because I knew the millionaire personally; I might
not even know more than my friend about the outward course of
the actions which revealed his character. For example, my friend
might live in the district in which the hospital had been built; he
might have watched it going up; he might have been inside it and
know better than I what kind and size of hospital it was. The point
is that to him, looking at it from outside, the building of the hospital
would have appeared just one more building operation like all the
others going on in the vicinity, and the hospital itself just one more,
added to all the others already existing in the area. What *I* should
be able to do for him would be to take him behind the scenes, as it
were, and to show him that, viewed from the inside, this ordinary
building operation was entirely due to the initiative and generosity
of the millionaire, and so constituted an act of his which revealed a
great deal about his character and attitudes.

But then there is the question what exactly *did* it reveal about
him? So far we have accepted his actions at their face value, as
evidence of sympathy and generosity; but in fact we can all quite
easily think of other possible interpretations of them. They might,
for example, have been so many bids for a knighthood or a peerage,
or they might even have been based on subtle calculations connected with tax evasion. My original interpretation may seem the

most reasonable guess, but it is a guess, and no one can take us beyond the realm of guessing except the millionaire himself. If we are to *know* the purpose and meaning of these actions—what they reveal about him—the knowledge must come from the man himself, though it may reach us through one or more intermediaries.

Of course this analogy breaks down, as analogies always do, at innumerable points; but the general application will be clear enough. It is the basic assumption of the biblical writers—which normally they do not attempt to prove—that there exists one with whom we must all carry on a relationship of life-and-death importance both for ourselves and for the communities in which we live. They do not claim to have penetrated into heaven and seen God face to face; they make no attempt to give us an account of his home life. What they do is first to describe certain historical events, which from the outside usually look just like other past events and are fully amenable to critical study by the historian. But then the biblical writers claim to be able to take us behind the scenes and show us that seen from within these historical events were in a special sense acts of God—saving and self-revealing acts in which God broke through, as it were, to encounter and help certain of his creatures and through them to reach the rest.[2]

Since their ability to do all this can come, in the last resort, only from God himself, we are approaching here very close to the question of inspiration. "Inspiration" is a word with innumerable associations in Christian theology, not all of them entirely desirable. In particular it has habitually been used in connection with what is known as the "two-source theory" of our knowledge of God— the idea, that is, that we can know some things about God by our own unaided intellectual effort, while other, and more intimate, knowledge can come only by direct, and sheerly supernatural, revelation from God himself. This theory has been subjected to searching criticism by C. C. J. Webb, Dr Rawlinson, Dr Hodgson,

---

[2] I am aware that this formulation of the matter begs an important question. There are those who, in interpreting these events as revelatory, emphasize, not so much their being acts of God in a special sense, as the providential presence of witnesses inspired to see and proclaim the events of their time as originating in the will of God. In many ways I myself sympathize with this interpretation; but as the question was not immediately relevant to this discussion, I have deliberately begged it here. I hope to deal with it in a subsequent paper.

and many others both here and abroad,[3] and I mention it now only in an attempt to make clear what I do, and do not, mean by inspiration. The Church has always said, and will no doubt always want to say, that the biblical writers are "inspired", in the sense that their knowledge of the status and meaning of certain events as acts of God is somehow derived from God himself. But the word need imply nothing, as I use it, about the *mode* of the derivation, and it certainly need not presuppose the traditional dichotomy between "natural" and "revealed" knowledge. I should not even want to rule out the possibility that in certain cases biblical writers may have derived their insights through human intermediaries; for example, the writers of some of the historical books of the Old Testament may well have derived their interpretation of Israel's history from the teaching of the prophets or priests whose disciples they seem, in some cases, to have been.

In any case, it is here, over the question of the *meaning and purpose* of the acts of God in history, that my analogy finally breaks down. In that analogy, what my friend and I were trying to read off from the actions of the millionaire was the character and purposes of a *fellow human being*. It follows that, however subtle and tortuous his character and purposes might be, they would in principle be capable of being completely understood by us, if only we took sufficient trouble, and were sufficiently imaginative and acute. But when it is the character and purposes of God we are dealing with, things must be very different, for at least two reasons. In the first place, no one could *fully* understand the character and purposes of the all-holy God unless he were himself completely holy and sinless; and we have no reason to think the biblical writers were sinless in that sense. And secondly, the purposes of God revealed by his acts in history must be all of a piece with his eternal character and being; and therefore no human being could fully comprehend or reveal the meaning of God's acts unless he were privy to God's eternal being, as no man in this world can ever be. We cannot take religious truth and cut it up into sections and then claim that to Moses section A and Elijah section B was perfectly made known, and so on with all the prophets, priests, and wise men. The truth of God must form an integral whole. Human beings who see but a

3 See, e.g., Webb, *Problems in the Relation of God and Man*, Hodgson, *For Faith and Freedom*, Vol. I, iv.

fragment of it can at best offer a fragmentary and imperfect interpretation of what they see. And it is important to realize that this is not an accidental fact, but something which belongs essentially to existence at the level of the creature, for human language and thought-forms are essentially geared to the limited existence of this world.

Before attempting to assess the implications of this, we shall do well to notice another, allied, inadequacy in my analogy. According to the analogy, the man whose actions my friend and I sought to interpret was a contemporary. But change the analogy for a moment; suppose now that the man my friend was seeking to under-stand was not a contemporary, but, say, a wealthy philanthropist of the Egypt of the eighteenth dynasty; and suppose that his guide and informant was not I, but some Egyptian writer contemporary with the philanthropist. However full and precise the account given by this writer, it would surely present my friend with considerable problems of interpretation. For the rich man's intentions would inevitably be expounded in terms of assumptions, values, and cus-toms quite unfamliar to a modern Englishman. A good deal of learn-ing, imaginative sympathy, and what is sometimes called "trans-lation" would be necessary before my friend could begin to feel that he was getting inside the mind of the original philanthropist or of his interpreter. Once again, it is important to recognize that we are dealing here with an essential and inescapable feature of life lived at the historical level. When all allowances have been made for the unchanging continuity of "human nature",[4] the fact remains that no writer who lives in history can interpret anything—even the deep things of God—except in terms of the accepted assump-tions, values, and decencies of his time. He may be, as we say, "ahead of his time", but that is a relative thing; man in history must always be the child of *some* age and so he must always make things intelligible in terms of the culture of that age; the very phrase "make intelligible" must always be relative to some familiar and accepted terminology. Put it like this: God himself could not have enabled Isaiah to interpret the divine activity in terms immediately appropriate to his own and all subsequent generations. For the Hebrew language of the period simply did not contain words to

[4] I use quotation marks because this phrase itself is a question-begging abstraction.

express many of the ideas in terms of which the modern English-man interprets his environment; and in any case, had the necessary words been miraculously provided, the resultant message would have been unintelligible to the prophet himself and to all generations down to the twentieth century.

The point is familiar, and does not need labouring; we may pass to another. The biblical writers all belonged to what we call the ancient world, and, for a number of reasons, it is a fact about that world that people in it could not attain to the kind of scientific his-torical accuracy with regard to past events which is possible to-day. Indeed, such accuracy was so remote from them that, at any rate with regard to the distant past, they had no conception of it, or even desire for it. The relevance of that for our subject is obvious enough. Unless a supply of error-free historical information was miracu-lously piped into their consciousnesses, their account of the various historical events which they expound as revealing acts of God is bound very often to seem woefully unsatisfactory and inaccurate when judged by the standards of current historical practice. That must be true, unless, as I said, a certain amount of error-free historical information was supplied to them; but before we take up the challenge implicit in that last phrase, it may be well to pause and take stock of what has been said so far.

I have assumed of course that God *has* acted in history to reveal himself and to save the world, very much in the way the Bible pre-supposes. Granted that, I have hinted at an interpretation of the function of the biblical writers which would ascribe authority to what they wrote, and even claim inspiration for it, without claim-ing detailed inerrancy for it at any level. On this interpretation, we should expect not only historical and scientific error, but error in matters of religion; and as for the precise words of the biblical writers, we should expect always to have to apply to them the question so admirably formulated by Professor Hodgson: "What must the truth be, and have been, if it appeared like that to men who thought and wrote as they did?"[5] In fact this is an account of biblical authority which leaves the whole matter very fluid and assigns a considerable rôle and responsibility to the modern

[5] Dr Hodgson formulates the question in slightly different ways in several of his books. See, e.g., *For Faith and Freedom*, Vol. I, pp. 87-8.

interpreter in the process of getting to know God with the help and guidance of the biblical writers.

I make no apology for that; but I *am* anxious not to give the impression of limiting unduly the scope of what the biblical writers were concerned to do. They were not confined to describing and interpreting certain acts of God in history; to suggest that they were would be to disfranchise certain biblical writers almost entirely. They were in fact fully aware that this world-order, which formed the necessary context of God's redemptive acts, itself owes its origin to God, and is, and always will be, in relationship with him. Among the things they seek to do is to define that relationship and then to show what kind of conduct is appropriate to inhabitants of a world so related to God. Our thoughts turn naturally in this connection to the Wisdom Literature, but in reading it, and still more in reading such books as the New Testament epistles, we cannot help noticing how the understanding of man's relation to God as creature to creator is constantly illuminated, deepened, and indeed defined, by the recognition of God's redemptive acts in history and so of man's relation to him as redeemed sinner to saviour.

But to these and to all the other things the biblical writers sought to do, the same general considerations seem to be applicable. Indeed it is in this sphere that some of the things I have been saying find their clearest exemplification. Consider, for example, the author of Genesis seeking to give expression to his conviction that this world is, first and last and always, entirely dependent on the freely-willed activity of God. Clearly the purpose of God in creating and sustaining this world must reach out into his general being and purposes, and so be incapable of being fully comprehended by any of his creatures. And the relationships of the universe as a whole cannot be *literally* described in language and thought-forms designed only to deal with the internal relations inside it. How then did the author of Genesis arrive at what he wrote? Must he not in fact have started from the world as he knew it, and its relationship to God as revealed in his own experience and in the experience and tradition of his people? And when it came to expressing this relationship, what else could he do but make use of the creation mythology current in the near East of his day, modifying it wherever necessary to make it a better vehicle for the special insights vouchsafed in his particular history and that of his people? It hardly needs to be added that the current mythology he used was itself distilled from innumerable individual experiences of God and his relation with his creatures. And clearly what is true of the mythology of the beginning is equally true of the mythology of the last things—of biblical eschatology. Of course I have grossly oversimplified my account of the origin of the first few chapters of Genesis and attributed an impossible amount to a single individual; but if my account is broadly true, at any rate in principle, you will see why I talk of the position being fluid, and plead for a certain flexibility in our approach to the Bible.

By us this fluidity may be seen as inevitable if there was to be revelation at all in a limited world subject to the laws of historical change and development; and we may welcome it in practice as giving us room for manoeuvre. But our predecessors in the faith have for the most part taken a different view. Traditional Christianity, both Catholic and Protestant, has made far broader claims for the Bible than I have been doing, in respect of both authority and inspiration. It has taken inspiration to imply inerrancy, and an inerrancy which has usually been held to extend even to detailed points of history and science. It must be conceded, therefore, that the sort of view I have been propounding can make no claim to be the full traditional view; but a number of other things must be said, if that concession is to be seen in the right perspective.

To begin with, the traditional belief in inerrancy is a matter of custom rather than dogmatic definition, and of custom which is not itself based on any very clear biblical authority. Canon Charles Smyth, writing of the period before the rise of modern science, goes so far as to say: ". . . nobody really believed in the verbal inspiration of the Holy Scriptures until the geologists began to question it. Hitherto, broadly speaking, people believed everything they read in the Bible, in the same way that some people believe everything they read in the newspapers."[6] The Bible itself nowhere claims inerrancy nor is it by any means consistently implied in the way the biblical writers treat one another's texts. The Church has always believed that the Bible is inspired and authoritative, but it has never *defined* the inspiration and authority, at any rate in any formularies binding on members of the Church of England. Indeed,

[6] *Church and Parish*, p. 159.

in so far as the Report of Committee 1 of the recent Lambeth Conference constituted an attempt to bring this matter within the sphere of dogmatic definition, it was undoubtedly something of a novelty, so far as the Church of England is concerned.

Then there is a second point of cardinal importance. The general belief of earlier ages that the Bible was inerrant must always be seen in the light of the methods of biblical exegesis current in those ages. Passages of Scripture were believed to have meaning other than the literal, for example, allegorical or typological meanings. In practice it was often in respect of those meanings that a passage was claimed to be an inerrant source of divine revelation. Origen indeed went so far as to deny that some passages of Scripture have any literal sense at all, or at any rate any literal sense which is revelatory of God. In the light of these facts, we can see that the sting of the doctrine of inerrancy was to some extent drawn in practice. In fact Origen and scholars like him were more than half aware of the problems I have described, and their doctrine of the multiple sense of Scripture was their practical device for dealing with those problems and for creating that room for manoeuvre to which I have referred. In practice, therefore, the situation has always been more fluid than would appear if we concentrated exclusively on the formal theory of inspiration. Our modern fundamentalists usually ignore these compensating factors, and as a result they are no more the direct heirs of traditional teaching in this matter than I am. They are in fact "plus royalistes que le roi"![7]

As a matter of fact their view is read off neither from tradition, nor from the Bible itself. It is based on an *a priori* argument which would run, if it were explicitly formulated, something like this: "We know that the Bible is inspired because we find God speaking to us through it. But the God who speaks through it is the God of truth, so it would be natural for him to secure complete freedom from error in the means of his communication with men. Moreover he is a God of love, and so it would be natural for him to be concerned about our fears, and to give us the security that would

[7] In the course of the lecture I did not have time to develop this point, but it is one which needs, and deserves, to be developed fully. It should not be supposed that the idea of a multiple sense of Scripture was a peculiarity of Origen and a few like-minded eccentrics; in one form or another it dominated practically all patristic and medieval exegesis, and most protestant exegesis in the period before the rise of the "critical" study of the Bible.

come from possessing an inerrant statement of the promise and
conditions of salvation." Anyone can see how natural such an
assumption is, yet it *is* only an assumption, and it can never be too
strongly stressed that where God is concerned, *a priori* assumptions
are always hazardous. How can any theist say what God "must"
have done, or know what is "natural" to him, seeing that he is
speaking of a being *toto caelo* different from himself? And if every
theist should hesitate before making such *a priori* statements about
what God "must" have done, how much more the Christian theist!
For if there is one thing the Bible and the history of the Church
make crystal clear it is that our God is the God of the unexpected.
Who dares to say what "must" be natural for a God who chose to
save through the chequered, and often ignominious, history of an
obscure little people in Palestine and the criminal's death of his
own Son? If the means of salvation involve the "scandal of
particularity", why not the means of publishing that salvation?
And in the light of the Bible and of Christian history, what are we to
say of the belief that God will surely be concerned to give us full
security? Can there be any doubt what must be said?

But if all this is true, how came the Church to maintain the idea
of biblical inerrancy so long? That is a question which up to a
point is readily answered, and the general lines of the answer are
familiar enough. For a long time the customs and assumptions of
western European man were so like those of biblical man that the
difficulties in the inerrancy position did not declare themselves with
their full force. I do not want to traverse well-worn ground again,
but I should like to emphasize how very recent are the really wide
divergences from the outlook of the biblical writers, of which we
are so conscious to-day. Professor C. S. Lewis has pointed out in his
Inaugural Lecture at Cambridge[8] that it is in the period after about
1800, and not at the Renaissance, that we must locate the really
major break in the cultural history of Europe. And Dr Charles
Galton Darwin writes as follows in his fascinating book on the next
million years:[9] ". . . during the last one hundred and fifty years, the
whole manner of living has been more changed than in the previous
fifteen hundred years. It is true that life in Western Europe in 1750
was very materially different from life in A.D. 100 in Italy; . . . there

8 *De Descriptione Temporum.* See especially pp. 11 & 18.
9 *The Next Million Years,* p. 49.

were important changes . . . but, without belittling these changes, they were on an incomparably smaller scale than those witnessed between 1750 and 1950, in nearly all parts of the world. It would surely be just to say that London in 1750 was far more like Rome in A.D. 100 than like either London or Rome in 1950." It is then only since the middle of the eighteenth century that we have begun to make the really fantastic advances in knowledge to which we are now accustomed, and that Christians have found themselves holding views and presuppositions on almost every subject markedly divergent from those of the biblical writers. And there is another point at least equally significant. It was only with this rapid divergence of world-view that there came, really for the first time, the consciousness how unlike one another men of different epochs are. It was this realization that gave rise, and such wide currency, to the historical novels*of Scott and to the work of historians like Lord Macaulay who were fired by them. We find it hard to realize, but up till the eighteenth century an almost completely static view of history prevailed, and much even of eighteenth-century thought was based on such a view. The theory of the social contract, for example, was formulated by men who took it for granted that human beings had always been rational creatures like themselves. And only recently we have been reminded that Coleridge was the first person to use the word "anachronism" in its modern sense. The magnitude of the changes we all realize; for our purposes their novelty is also important.

These changes were enough in themselves to alter men's orientation to the Bible, but in fact of course they were reinforced by the conclusions of the growing army of biblical critics, armed with all the weapons and techniques of research that the new developments had put at their disposal. Specific inaccuracies in the received text were thus pin-pointed, and it became clear that, whatever the truth of the Bible, the terms and thought-forms in which the biblical writers formulated it were simply the common coin of the philosophy and religion of a particular age. All this is really of very recent occurrence, and that may help to explain why the general considerations I advanced in the first part of this lecture, although they applied just as much before 1750 as they do now, did not impress themselves on Christians of an earlier period. It may also prevent our being too worried by our divergence in this matter from traditional views. The revolution that began in the eighteenth century was fundamental and far-reaching. Its implications were bound to take time to seep through, so it is only to be expected that ours should be one of the first generations of Christians to be faced with the need for a reappraisal which may well be not only agonizing but prolonged; for certainly at the moment the modern revolution shows no signs of having spent itself. And, that being so, it is only natural that our attitude to the authority and inspiration of the Bible should be very different from that of the Fathers, the Schoolmen, the Protestant Reformers, or even the eighteenth-century Latitudinarians and their opponents.

What then should our attitude be? Certainly there is no lack of suggestions nowadays from theologians of every school. The position which most commended itself to the Lambeth Bishops seems to have been that which they describe as "Biblical Theology". Whatever precisely is meant by that term,[10] it clearly refers to a view which holds that, when all allowances have been made for the historical and theological limitations of the biblical writers, their accounts, even as they stand, enshrine a hard core of truth, both historical and theological. The key events of their story—the Exodus, the entering into the Promised Land, the apostasy under the kings, the consequent Exile and the rest—all happened substantially as the biblical writers relate; and if we follow the broad lines of their interpretation, we can trace a single line of divine policy running through these successive events, a coherent plan of salvation which culminated in the ministry of Christ and the foundation of the Church. Sometimes the internal testimony of the Holy Spirit is invoked as the authority for selecting just *this* line of events as the key episodes in the Biblical story, and the exponents of Biblical Theology usually suggest that, at any rate as far as these key incidents are concerned, the categories of the biblical writers themselves are wholly adequate for their interpretation, if not indeed the only ones legitimate for the purpose.[11] It will be clear from what I

[10] The words "Biblical Theology" have been applied to a variety of views, and it is a pity that the Lambeth Report does not define more precisely how it understands the term.

[11] The Lambeth Committee Report suggests the use of the category of *drama* to supplement and illuminate the other categories employed by Biblical Theology. For a critique of this suggestion see *The York Quarterly*, for November 1958, pp. 4-5.

have already said how far I am in sympathy with this approach; yet I do not think it can be accepted by any means without qualification, particularly if it is offered as a total solution of the problem of the modern approach to the Bible. In the first place, as I hinted earlier, it is in danger of disfranchising large sections of the Bible; significantly, the exposition of it in the Lambeth Report has very little to say about the New Testament, and particularly about the New Testament epistles. The necessity of appealing to the internal witness of the Spirit suggests that this approach is in fact highly selective, and often it is not as true to the general proportions of the Bible itself as its exponents seem to suppose. All of which leads me on to a deeper doubt. Can it be that some, at any rate, of the exponents of Biblical Theology are motivated by the old longing for security? Are they perhaps trying to isolate *some* element in the Bible which can be shown to need neither historical revision nor theological reinterpretation? Any such attempt is surely doomed to failure, and even to make it involves serious temptations. With regard to the historical accuracy of the biblical narratives, some biblical theologians sometimes seem to me already to be on the verge of treating the problems *a priori* and sitting a shade loose to the empirical evidence. For example, I have sometimes heard it treated simply as a matter for derision that the historicity of Moses should be questioned; and the whole question is frequently shrugged off with the epigram: "If Moses had not existed it would be necessary to invent him." The Biblical Theologians may well be right about this particular issue, on the evidence at present available—I am not sufficient of an expert in Old Testament matters to know; but the question is not one which can be settled by any other method than the patient, detailed examination of historical evidence, in the full realization that subsequent discoveries and developments may compel a complete change of opinion. The point I want to make is that a search for final security in a sphere where imperfectly-attested historical events are involved is foredoomed to failure.

As for the insistence on interpreting the biblical events exclusively in the categories used by the biblical writers themselves, such ancient Semitic and Hellenistic categories are not the natural ones for the modern European to use, and he can only confine himself to them at the cost of ignoring a number of questions which inevitably occur to him. Professor Cullmann and other exponents of Biblical Theology do in fact demand of us just such a self-denying ordinance, and as a result they are able to attribute to the categories of the Bible a more or less absolute validity. In this way they gain a confident security with regard to the biblical revelation— they know exactly what it means, but it is at the cost of writing "improper" across a whole area of what is apparently perfectly proper inquiry and valid insight. Professor Hodgson has dealt very faithfully with this question in his recent Gifford Lectures,[12] so I will leave it with just one quotation from what he there says: "It is, of course, true that the revelation given to us through the Bible comes through Hebrew minds, and that questions which troubled the Greek thinkers apparently never occurred to them. But to draw from this the conclusion that God wills us neither to raise these questions nor to seek to learn from those who have thought profoundly about them is ludicrously absurd. Why, in order to be a good Christian should it be more important to have a Hebrew type of mind than to have a Hebrew cast of countenance? If we must be limited to the Jewish idea of eternity, why not to the Jewish shape of nose?"

Biblical Theology then, is a good servant but a bad master. As a suggestion of one very fruitful way of approaching the Bible, it has a lot to commend it; but when it claims a monopoly of the field, it reveals another side, on which it has some at least of the characteristics of a failure of nerve.

Much the same must be said about the approach to the Bible associated with the names of Dr Austin Farrer and Dr Lionel Thornton. These scholars rightly point out that Hebrew thought usually proceeded, not so much by way of systematic argument as by the accumulation of successive images which would suggest different aspects of the truth, and the interweaving of them in such a way as to preserve the balance and proportions of the whole. From this come most valuable insights about how at any rate certain biblical passages should be approached and unravelled. Yet here again we cannot allow such an appreciation to be converted into a total theory of biblical authority. Dr Hodgson writes:[13] "There are passages in Dr Austin Farrer's Bampton Lectures[14] which

---

12 *For Faith and Freedom;* see Vol. I, p. 78.
13 Ibid., Vol. I, p. 76.   14 *The Glass of Vision.*

seem to suggest that the presentation of truth in images is what constitutes the Bible a revelation of divine truth. Taken by itself this book suggests . . . that it is the presentation in images that makes the Bible revelatory and that if we would receive God's revelation we must think in images too." I am not quite sure that that does full justice to Dr Farrer's book; and I *am* quite sure that I have not done justice to a way of approaching the Bible which I myself have found very illuminating, and for which I am extremely grateful. Yet I think I see Dr Hodgson's point, and I sympathize with him. He is worried by the tendency to pin-point the authority of the Bible in any one aspect of, or element in, it. In the old days, if Christians were asked, "Wherein does the authority of the Bible lie?" they could answer, "In the inerrant truth of all its state-ments". Now that that answer is no longer possible, there is a natural temptation to try to find some equally simple alternative answer. For example: "Its authority lies in the image character of its thinking and in the content and mutual interplay of its images. Allow that hierarchy of images to condition your response to God and your neighbour and all will certainly be well." Or: "Base your relation to God and the world on the belief that the key incidents of the biblical theologian actually took place and meant what the Bible says they did, and again all will be well." Of course I caricature, but you will see my point. The question about biblical authority can be simply formulated, and it is always a temptation to assume that questions which can be simply formulated must have answers capable of equally simple formulation. But that is a temptation to which we should not always succumb. And in this case the very amorphous and heterogeneous character of the biblical material might suggest that it is not meant to yield up its secret in any one easily formulable way.

So perhaps the best thing I can say in reply to your question, "Wherein does the authority of the Bible lie?" is that it is a deceptively simple question. Beware of all who claim to have a simple answer to it; they are almost certainly guilty of serious, and dangerous, oversimplification. At any rate at the present stage this is a problem which *solvitur ambulando*; obviously the clue must be found in the figure and work of Jesus, on which all else converges, but as we try to use that clue we shall become increasingly aware that the problem of biblical authority cannot be cleared up in isolation. The authority of the Bible is inextricably connected with other authorities — the authority of the Church, of the saints, of the liturgy, the conscience, and the reason.